THE
INNOVATION
KILLER

THE
INNOVATION
KILLER

● ● ● ● ● ● ● ● ● ● ● ● ● ●

HOW WHAT WE KNOW

LIMITS WHAT WE CAN IMAGINE . . .

AND WHAT SMART COMPANIES

ARE DOING ABOUT IT

CYNTHIA BARTON RABE

AMACOM

AMERICAN MANAGEMENT ASSOCIATION

New York • Atlanta • Brussels • Chicago • Mexico City • San Francisco
Shanghai • Tokyo • Toronto • Washington, D.C.

Special discounts on bulk quantities of AMACOM books are
available to corporations, professional associations, and other
organizations. For details, contact Special Sales Department,
AMACOM, a division of American Management Association,
1601 Broadway, New York, NY 10019.
Tel.: 212-903-8316.   Fax: 212-903-8083.
Web Site: www.amacombooks.org

This publication is designed to provide accurate and authoritative
information in regard to the subject matter covered. It is sold with the
understanding that the publisher is not engaged in rendering legal,
accounting, or other professional service. If legal advice or other
expert assistance is required, the services of a competent professional
person should be sought.

Library of Congress Cataloging-in-Publication Data

Rabe, Cynthia Barton.
    The innovation killer : how what we know limits what we can imagine : and what
smart companies are doing about it / Cynthia Barton Rabe.
        p.   cm.
    Includes index.
    ISBN-10: 0-8144-0883-4
    ISBN-13: 978-0-8144-0883-4
    1. Creative ability in business.   2. Creative thinking.   3. Problem solving.
4. Organizational effectiveness.   I. Title.

HD53.R33   2006
658.4'063—dc22

                                                          2005037125

Printing number

10   9   8   7   6   5   4   3   2   1

To my husband Jim and my daughter Katy, who make home my favorite place to be, and to my parents, Carl and Barbara Barton, who taught me how to make my own luck.

CONTENTS

····················

FOREWORD
....

REMEMBER THE INNOVATION-INTOXICATED years of 1999-2000? New ideas for Internet applications were so thick in the air that MBA students fled school mid-year to stake claims in cyberspace. Gray-haired executives packed up their mahogany-paneled Midwest offices and squeezed into tiny cubicles housing company startups. Wags said at the time that anyone who could power up a computer to present a new business idea could get funding from venture capitalists. After the euphoria of the boom and the depression of the bust passed, we had all received some painful reminders about the nature of innovation. Innovation is a balancing act: between expertise and beginner's mind; respect for immutable laws of human behavior and irreverence for historical precedent; focused chaos and structured systems. When the innovative attempt tips too far toward what has worked before, we get stagnation; when unbridled enthusiasm overrides common sense, we get emperors with no clothes—products and businesses without substance.

This book presents a way to manage that balancing act, to both draw on expertise and also challenge it. My first thought on reading it was that it pulled together two related but different fields of research in which I've immersed myself—creativity and the development of what my coauthor and I call "deep smarts"—experience-based skills and knowledge. I was intrigued by Rabe's "zero-gravity thinkers" because she has put her finger on a very important interaction between the two. In over thirty years of working on innovation, I've encountered many of the notions about creativity contained herein before. For example, the idea that creative thought occurs at intersections is not new. It is no accident that the Renaissance flourished at a geographical crossroads in Europe, or that in recent history, the popularity of cross-functional teams has grown exponentially. Other authors (myself included) have written about the virtues of creating collisions of thought that yield innovation—abrasion for creative purposes. Moreover, such writers have suggested the value of introducing people sometimes termed "aliens" into the innovative process, so that they may infuse fresh thinking and spur creative abrasion. So what is new here? The new ideas contained in this volume revolve around collaboration with a *particularly valuable kind* of alien—Zero-Gravity Thinkers. I know of no one else who has described this type of collaborator—much less provided the solid, practical guidance in identifying and utilizing them that this book does.

As Rabe's many examples show, aliens in general are valuable. Innovation, whether it be in new products and services, unusual organizational processes, new systems or any other novel activity, profits from the presence of creative abrasion, i.e., intellectual disagreement. An innovating team may rely upon long-held assumptions or, at the other extreme, become so enamored of a novelty that they fail to ask appropriate questions about its appeal and significance. (In the initial Internet boom, aggregating eyeballs was deemed an indication of success, whether or not anyone took out a credit card to buy something.) Useful aliens tend to ask profoundly simple questions and to see unexpected complications in the road ahead. They are also adept at identifying opportunities and suggesting unusual connections.

We owe much progress in science, technology, and medicine to aliens. For example, the field of psycho-neuroimmunology owes its very existence to a psychologist, Robert Ader, who started working with immunologist Nicolas Cohen in the 1970s. At the time, the immune system was believed to be one region of the body that operated independently of the brain. In the course of laboratory experiments, Ader stumbled across evidence suggesting that rats continued to be vulnerable to disease long after the initial conditioning response that involved a temporary suppression of the immune systems. No one working in immunology was interested in this unorthodox view, coming as it did from a totally unrelated knowledge field. But one immunologist listened to the alien. Nicholas Cohen was willing to test the hypothesis. Over thirty years later, researchers are still on the track of the biological mechanisms that connect the brain and the immune system, but the field is well established. In fact, the initial idea proposed by the alien is so well accepted that one problem he faces now is exaggerated claims that reduction in stress can cure all diseases.

Ader was not a naïf—nor was Cohen. They were both deeply smart—experts in their own fields. It was the blend of their different forms of expertise that yielded the innovation. And they were both scientists, so they did have some common language. But, as in the case of so many instances of scientific and technical innovation, there was an element of serendipity to this story. Cohen did not seek out Ader in order to challenge the prevailing assumptions about the nature of the immune system. And Ader didn't set out to stretch prevailing paradigms. The world is fortunate that Ader persisted and Cohen listened. But, this book asks, how can we introduce more of this kind of serendipity into our innovation processes? What if we could figure out how to infuse our organizations with enough Zero-Gravity Thinkers to consistently incite challenges to our assumptions when we are trying to solve really important problems?

We would all like to believe that we can challenge our own assumptions. But that is hard enough on an individual basis. ("I'm too old or too young, too clumsy or too busy to. . . . you can fill in the blank.) It is even more difficult within a fairly cohesive group and inside an organization. Birds who flock together do become more of a feather. So we need the outsider to ask the questions that we will not. The Zero-Gravity-Thinkers characteristics describe people whom we can respect. They have expertise in a related field—so they have a proven track record; they have earned their spurs. They are not in competition with us for the same rewards, so we do not lose by using their advice. And they ask questions that make us think—possibly annoy us, but intellectually rather than personally.

It is tricky to manage the creative abrasion that such aliens inspire. For many people, intellectual disagreement is difficult to separate from personal annoyance. Moreover, such collaborators will appear to slow the process—in fact they *will* slow the process. But if speed and efficiency are more important than innovation, then you don't want to invite Zero-Gravity Thinkers in to begin with.

Zero-Gravity Thinkers do not abound. For starters, research shows that it takes seven to ten years to develop true expertise, whether in bread-making or skiing, hiring winning salespeople, or laying bricks. Therefore such collaborators are likely to be highly valuable within their own disciplines, and costly to loan out to play the role of gadfly. Moreover, renaissance thinking is rare. But we don't need these rare thinkers on every project. One of the biggest mistakes that managers can make is to staff and manage all projects—even all innovation projects—exactly alike. Radical innovation requires a very different team from incremental innovation.

But what if you don't think you have any Zero-Gravity Thinkers in your group or organization? As Rabe reports, research indicates that people exposed to many different kinds of environments and learning opportunities are more likely to be creative thinkers. Managers should consider stimulating more renaissance thinking in their groups. Best Buy CEO Brad Anderson did just that when he set up a budget for his rather insular organization to learn how to innovate better, and financed a consulting firm to work with thirty-five of his mid-level managers for six months, to transfer innovative processes and thinking. The managers went through exhilarating and painful experiences. For example, one of the managers, Toby Nord, found that his mind was stretched by visiting the American Girl store in Chicago. This store, which sells historic dolls to little girls (and their mothers and grandmothers) was not a comfortable place for a male. But it was an experience! Nord and his fellow team members had a number of revelations from seeing that this retail site was much more than a store; it was a destination. There were doll-centric activities such as stations for styling the dolls' hair, and a cafeteria where the dolls were seated at the tables and the menu included specially named foods. The Best Buy visitors were surprised to see people posing outside the store to have their pictures taken. The dolls provided a cross-generational platform for communication and entertainment.

Subsequently, Nord visited Mexico, the Amish countryside in the United States, and Korea, being bombarded with new stimuli on each trip. Although untrained in anthropology or sociology, he began to make connections about human behavior among the sites visited—e.g., the human desire for identity with a community. He began to question some of the long-held Best Buy assumptions about what constitutes a store, a product line, or a customer profile. Even when he was on vacation, he saw the world differently and brought an inquiring mind to activities in airports and social gatherings. He had developed more of a renaissance mind. Best Buy has profited handsomely from Brad Anderson's investment in such individuals. Innovative thinking is permeating the organization in ways it simply did not five years ago, resulting in new businesses, new store concepts—even new management structures. As this case suggests, managers can provide stimuli to stretch the mind, although of course there are many less expensive ways of doing so.

Another source of the diverse experiences that aid in renaissance thinking is job movement within an organization. When individuals are caught in silos, i.e., narrowly defined roles, they do not have a chance to stretch their minds. Gifted people leave because they cannot move to a position that gives them a fresh perspective. In such organizations, a person once marked as "financial," for example, finds it impossible to move into manufacturing—even though experience in operations would likely make him much more valuable to the organization in the future. Innovative organizations have more porous boundaries and less rigid attitudes toward job descriptions.

When I entered the field of innovation several decades ago, researchers and managers believed that every new product designed and implemented was essentially a one-off project. At the time, as strange as it may seem now, no one argued that new product development could be systematized. Over the years, we have learned how to put more structure and consistent activities into the new product development process. Many companies have portfolios of projects, managed through various different types of stage-gate processes. We have also added some predictability to the invention process. Wise managers are careful not to place too much structure or financial constraints on highly innovative projects, but only the smallest, one-product companies can eschew all repeatable processes. But the search for ways to manage innovation extends beyond new product development. Some of us maintain that even the process of creativity itself—applied to *any* problem or innovative opportunity—can be managed and encouraged, albeit not totally controlled. The design consultants IDEO mentioned in this book exemplify such a process. So as we develop more understanding of the dynamics of innovation, we render it more manageable, more consistently attainable.

The suggestion that Zero-Gravity Thinkers can enhance the innovation process is another advance in the effort to enhance the probability of success. Like many of the advances in the theory of innovation, the idea is not subject to immediate cost-benefit analysis. Too much depends upon its execution. However, this idea is well supported by research on human behavior in general and on innovative behavior specifically. And it provides one more tool that managers can systematically apply to the innovation journey.

Dorothy A. Leonard
Professor Emerita, Harvard Business School
Author, *When Sparks Fly*

ACKNOWLEDGMENTS

I WOULD LIKE TO ACKNOWLEDGE the many people who have helped me complete this work. I'll start by thanking my sister, Linda Barton Chambliss, for spending countless hours tracking reference sources and acquiring copyright permissions. Her assistance and persistence has been invaluable and incredibly appreciated.

I would also like to thank the friends and colleagues who read and commented on various versions of the manuscript prior to its completion: Barry Bonder, Linda Bonder, Rob Chapman, Rick Coulson, Herman D'Hooge, Wayne Embree, Dave Garten, Dorothy Leonard, Scott Page, Jack Raiton, Shane Wall, Richard Watson, and Jan Wolfe. To call it a favor to read someone's (or at least my) unfinished manuscript draft would be an understatement. Their generous contribution of time and intellect to this effort led to countless improvements.

Finally, I want to thank the people who shared their innovation stories and insights with me. They have been cited throughout the book, but it is important to acknowledge that their willingness to talk with me added new dimensions to my thinking, which I hope are conveyed in the following pages.

For all of this help and support, as well as the encouragement and guidance I received from the folks at AMACOM, particularly from Editor-in-Chief Adrienne Hickey, I am very grateful.

INTRODUCTION

A CRUSHING FORCE

WE FACE A DILEMMA. When it comes to innovation, the same hard-won experience, best practices, and processes that are the cornerstones of an organization's success may be more like millstones that threaten to sink it. Said another way, the weight of what we know, especially what we collectively "know," kills innovation. Yet in many fields what we must know in order to make even the most basic contribution is ever-increasing.

• THE PARADOX OF EXPERTISE •

It is a paradox. The Paradox of Expertise. You can't innovate with it. You can't innovate without it.

Why can knowledge and experience be so lethal to innovation?

> ►The Paradox of Expertise
>
> You Can't Innovate with It.
>
> You Can't Innovate Without It. ■

Because when we become expert, we often trade our "what if" flights of fancy for the grounded reality of "what is." But insight and innovation require a certain lightness of mind. Perhaps Wilbur and Orville Wright, two brothers with high-school educations who earned their living building bicycles, didn't know enough to realize they were attempting the impossible when they first defied gravity in a powered aircraft on December 17, 1903 in Kitty Hawk, North Carolina. If they had been the recipients of more formal education, would they have had the attitude that Orville illustrates with this quote? "If we worked on the assumption that what is accepted as true really is true, then there would be little hope for advance." Perhaps not.

Noted economist and Princeton professor emeritus, William J. Baumol, wrote a paper entitled "Education for Innovation," outlining the negative impact formal education can have on innovative thinking capability because it so completely indoctrinates individuals in the expert thinking of a field. He notes that many breakthrough inventions are the work of individuals who have relatively low levels of formal training. Citing the Wright Brothers as well as other relatively under-formally-educated examples—such as Bill Gates, Thomas Edison, and Steve Jobs—Baumol introduces the hypothesis that education meant to help a student master a subject might be completely at odds with fostering innovation in that subject.[1]

Now contrast this caution against overeducation with the obvious fact that without increasing levels of knowledge there would be no progress. Professor Benjamin Jones of Northwestern University recalls Isaac Newton's famous words of 1676, "If I have seen further it is by standing on the shoulders of giants." He then notes that "if one is to stand on the shoulders of giants, one must first climb up on their backs, and the greater the body of knowledge, the harder this climb becomes." He asserts that over time the educational burden will continue to increase as would-be innovators strive to learn what their predecessors knew and then go beyond it. As one proof-point of this assertion he notes that the average age at which great inventors and Nobel Prize winners introduced their "great innovations" increased by six years during the last century.[2]

This statistic isn't difficult to believe. Few would argue that modern aeronautics engineers need to know everything the Wright Brothers did plus the knowledge accumulated in over a century since then in order to contribute meaningfully to the development of new airplanes. Or, that the knowledge required to invent the wheel was minuscule compared to that required to build a Toyota Prius or a Mercedes Benz today. Or, even that business managers need to have a deeper understanding of organizational science, manufacturing techniques, and financial models than the business owners of earlier generations.

Where does this bring us? Back to the paradox. If the weight of what we know kills innovation then it also supports it. As with so many things, the trick is in the balance. Though Wilbur and Orville sought to defy gravity, they would undoubtedly have recognized its necessity. In fact, it is likely they were even grateful that its pull kept their fledgling aircraft from floating irretrievably to the heavens once it left the Earth's surface.

Of course, what the Wright Brothers were dealing with was a consistent force of nature. But in many ways organizations have an advantage. They have the ability to set their own gravity dial. Through process, culture, and team mix they can, to a large extent, determine the level of force that "what they know" exerts on the system.

The problem is that many organizations have turned the dial

to an almost crushing level. In an effort to make our teams as efficient and effective as possible, we seek to staff them with those who have deep knowledge and proven capabilities in our fields. We look for the best and the brightest. Those who have earned the most prestigious academic credentials, received the most glowing professional accolades, and attained the most visible successes in fields most relevant to ours are highly sought after. And, when they join our ranks, we give them our full attention. The greater their perceived expertise in fact, the more we allow them to influence our thinking. Most of the time, this is a good thing. Experts, after all, frequently know what they are talking about.

The danger lies in our obsession. Many of us have taken our regard for the expert—and even for our own expertise—too far. Our esteem for deep knowledge has relegated the intuitive generalist, the creative novice, and even the "expert-in-a-field-other-than-what-we-are-interested-in-at-the-moment," to second-class status. The result? A lost ability to defy "gravity."

But this doesn't need to continue. We have the power to reset the "gravity" dial. We can, for instance, follow the advice of such innovation masters as industrial design firm IDEO. In the book, *The Ten Faces of Innovation*, by IDEO's general manager Tom Kelley, readers are encouraged to build diverse workgroups keeping in mind the various types of people required to optimize innovation efforts. We can also follow the recommendations of such noted academics as Stanford's Robert Sutton, who wrote *Weird Ideas That Work*. Establishing a culture that occasionally operates counter to traditional management "wisdom" can be surprisingly liberating from the standpoint of innovation. There are, in fact, numerous other sources of outstanding advice for lightening the expertise load. What most of this advice has in common, however, is the assumption that we can rid ourselves of this burden on our own.

I submit that sometimes a self-help approach isn't enough. After working for and with some of the best companies in the world (and I mean *best* in every sense of the word—from performance to the quality of their employees), I am convinced that the weight of expertise may be so burdensome that when it comes to innovation outside help is sometimes required. And that's where Zero-Gravity Thinkers come in.

Zero-Gravity refers to the weightless conditions experienced by astronauts during space flight or by those of us brave enough (or with stomach enough) to participate in a parabolic flight—one of those roller coaster-like flights that simulate weightlessness. As the name suggests, *Zero-Gravity Thinkers* are outsiders who are not weighed down by the expertise of a team, its politics or "the way things have always been done." They are temporary team members with specific characteristics (outlined in detail in Part II of this book) who can help a team push beyond the limits of its existing mindset. Zero-Gravity Thinkers help us re-set the gravity dial in our organizations by helping us attain a degree of weightlessness ourselves.

At its heart this is a book about the micro-side of innovation. It makes no sweeping statements about strategy or sustainable competitive advantages. It offers no opinion on the wisdom of clinging to the core or searching for white spaces in which to expand. Those vital macro-issues are left to other books. There is, unfortunately, more than one potential innovation killer.

This is a book about the human side of innovation; the side that lends itself less to the hard and fast analysis that many leaders find most comfortable, and more to the nuanced realm of social science and even, yes . . . emotion. It is a book that attempts to remind us that every new invention, every great idea, every revolutionary concept is the product of a person or, more likely, a group of people. It is a book that suggests the time has come for us to reconsider some of our most fundamental beliefs about who can add value when it comes to generating these insights because what we know, how we have been conditioned to work, even what we want to achieve, all tether us to what has been and constrain our ability to see what might be. In our ongoing quest for improvement, this book suggests that we must escape the crushing force of "what we know" and introduces Zero-Gravity Thinkers as a way for us to do it.

• AN OVERVIEW OF THE BOOK STRUCTURE •

This book is organized in three parts. Part I outlines the reasons innovative thinking (and therefore, innovation) is so difficult in organizations. It presents the argument, based on extensive research and anecdotal information, that human nature itself is the obstacle that must be overcome. Although the concepts in Part I may be familiar, they are worth reviewing as they set the stage for the rest of the book.

Part II introduces the three characteristics of the Zero-Gravity Thinker: psychological distance, renaissance tendencies, and related expertise. It builds an argument for why each is important in helping teams overcome the obstacles of human nature where innovation is concerned.

Part III is the "how to" portion of the book. It suggests how to work with a Zero-Gravity Thinker. It also introduces ways to achieve "weightless thinking" when a Zero-Gravity Thinker is not part of the team.

• A NOTE ON TERMINOLOGY •

Throughout the book I often use the words "team," "group," "organization," and "company" interchangeably to refer to a collection of people working toward finding a solution to a challenge. Except where noted or obvious, there is no significance to the use of one term versus another.

I also frequently use the words "challenge" and "problem" to describe the issue around which a team is attempting to generate innovative insights. This word choice isn't meant to suggest that I believe innovation is always in response to a negative. I could just as easily have chosen "opportunity" in many instances, and I beg the indulgence of my marketing colleagues, who tend to prefer this more positive word.

PART I

....

WHAT'S WEIGHING US DOWN

The intuitive mind is a sacred gift and the rational mind is a faithful servant. We have created a society that honors the servant and has forgotten the gift. —*Albert Einstein*

Let's start this book by examining how and why we do this. Chapter 1 outlines the challenges human nature introduces into the innovation process, and discusses the origins of the Zero-Gravity-Thinker concept. Chapter 2 provides an in-depth look at Groupthink, one of our best understood, but most commonly practiced innovation-constraining behaviors. And Chapter 3 details ExpertThink, the tendency we have individually and organizationally to stick with "what we know"—an anti-innovation recipe if ever there was one. This portion of the book outlines the problem. The rest of the book focuses on solving it.

CHAPTER 1

OUR OWN WORST ENEMY

HOW THE BURDEN OF WHAT WE KNOW
LIMITS WHAT WE CAN IMAGINE

> A number of studies show that people are less
> likely to make optimal decisions after prolonged
> periods of success. NASA, Enron, Lucent,
> WorldCom—all had reached the mountaintop
> before they ran into trouble. Someone should have
> told them that most mountaineering accidents
> happen on the way down. — *Ram Charan, Jerry
> Useem, Fortune Magazine, May 27, 2002*

ANTICIPATION IS ALMOST PALPABLE in New York's
Lincoln Center today. To those just entering, the radiant energy
inside the center's Rose Hall offers a sharp contrast to the clouds
and monsoon-like rain of last night. Throngs of people bustle about
with purpose, many undoubtedly readying themselves for a day
they expect to invigorate and even change them. What I have
stepped into is *Fortune* Magazine's 2005 Innovation Conference.
And, perhaps, what is palpable is not anticipation, but hope.

Innovation is a hot topic. With good reason. Increasingly, what
companies in the United States and other economically mature
countries are finding is that their counterparts in economically
emerging countries (China, India, Russia, etc.) are quickly gaining

the ability to offer comparable products and services better, faster, and cheaper than they can. *BusinessWeek* proposed in a recent article that the age of the "Knowledge Economy" is quickly giving way to what they call the "Creative Economy."[1] It will not, the article suggests, be knowledge that differentiates companies in the future—that playing field is leveling—but the ability to offer new, creative, and innovative products and services. Regardless of whether this global economic sea-change is a conscious consideration—or even the primary one—executives have dived into the innovation current headfirst. In a recent poll by *McKinsey Quarterly*, top U.S. executives cited the most important factor for growth in their organizations as the ability to innovate.[2]

It's no wonder then that conferences like the one at Lincoln Center are packed. It's also not surprising that almost daily a new article or book is introduced on the subject. We all feel the pressing need to unlock the secrets that will allow us to innovate because so few of us seem to know how. Or, maybe it's more accurate to say that few of us know how to sustain it in our organizations once we've had an initial taste of it.

Why is it so hard? Why, when we attend these conferences and read every one of the latest books and articles—and then faithfully execute their theories—do we so often fall short? My very un-politically correct opinion is that we are handicapped. We are innately disadvantaged when it comes to fostering ongoing innovative thinking in our organizations. And, as it turns out, human nature itself is at the root of the problem.

● FIRST THINGS FIRST: ●
WHAT EXACTLY IS INNOVATION?

But first things first. Before we talk about innovative thinking, let's define *innovation*. Though it seems pretty straightforward, I've run across dozens of definitions and never seem to get quite the same answer from different people I talk to on the subject.

"So, you're writing about ways to come up with new technology products, huh?" a friend of mine at Intel asked when I told him I was writing a book about innovation.

"No," was my response. "At least I'm not writing only about ways to come up with new technology products."

The truth is, my friend's technology/product-oriented definition of innovation is all too common but way too narrow. In business innovations occur all of the time in every function from manufacturing and marketing to customer service and finance. In fact, to get a feel for the link between innovation and various business functions, I decided to conduct a little unscientific test. My theory is that the more the word "innovation" gets paired with a functional word like "engineering" or "finance" in publications, the more likely it is that people in that field are interested in innovating.

With that in mind, I entered the words innovation and engineering in Google and found a whopping 7.1 million references. Innovation and manufacturing brought up over 5 million. And even a search of innovation and accounting (not a function I typically think of as terribly innovative) brought up an impressive 2.5 million references. My point is that innovation is not limited to products and technologies.

The introduction of the Energizer Bunny advertising campaign in 1989, in which the bunny "interrupted" fake television advertisements for such mundane products as pain relievers or allergy medicine, was a highly successful marketing innovation by advertising agency Chiat/Day (Figure 1-1).

Amazon's use of the Internet (initially for retailing books and then for peddling a host of other products) has been a phenomenal retailing, or e-tailing, innovation. And Intel's continuous breakthroughs in manufacturing have been innovations as instrumental in its success as its electrical engineering developments.

Outside of business, innovations abound in medicine, government, cooking, and art—the list is endless. Even innovation and legal practice referenced 2.1 million pages on Google! Plain and simple, we humans try to do everything better.

With this in mind, I define *innovation* as follows:

Innovation is
the application of an idea
that results in a valuable improvement.

Figure 1-1. The Energizer Bunny. ©Eveready Battery Company, Inc. 2004. Reprinted with permission.

A few respected colleagues have argued with me over this definition, saying that it is too broad. The word innovation, they assert, should be reserved for dramatic, disruptive, revolutionary improvements, not for evolutionary upgrades or simple modifications. I understand their point of view, but will respectfully disagree. Sometimes seemingly modest changes can have a significant impact. And whether a change is modest or dramatic is somewhat subjective.

Was it a modest or dramatic improvement when Starbucks (Figure 1-2), which as of this writing has a market capitalization in

Figure 1-2.

excess of $4 billion, started selling dark-roasted coffee served by baristas (just as Italians have been doing for years) instead of light-roasted coffee served by waiters (as Americans had been accustomed to)? Was it an evolution or a revolution when in 1913 the Ford Motor Company applied the concept of the conveyer belt, which canneries had been using since the late 1800s, to the manufacture of automobiles in what came to be called the assembly line? Was it a dramatic or simple change in 1982 when the Coca-Cola Company introduced a sugar-free cola to compete with Tab and called it Diet Coke? To the consumers worldwide who have made Diet Coke the 4th most popular carbonated soft drink in the world,[3] I don't think it matters.

The point is that an idea might be fresh and "innovative" to some people, but old hat to others. It might be a seemingly minor tweak to those "in the know," but one that makes all the difference to a customer. Few innovations simply materialize as if from nothing. And I would argue that those that do aren't necessarily any better than the ones that simply evolved. The opportunity is to establish a climate where any type of idea that might have value can flourish.

So, I'll go back to the definition I will use for the purposes of this book: *Innovation is the application of an idea that results in a valuable improvement.*

• THE ATTACK ON INNOVATIVE THINKING •

The point of the definition is to emphasize that the ability to think innovatively should be a goal for every function in an organization—not just the new product or technology development team. Consider this: Would you rather own stock in a company where all employees from new product development to finance and IT were encouraged to think of new and better ways to do things? Or would you prefer the company that only asked the new product developers to think out-of-the-box? This book is based on the premise that we'd all prefer the former.

Unfortunately, this book is also based on the premise that our ability to think innovatively within each and every function in an organization is under attack. And, the attack isn't coming from the outside. It's coming from within. Perhaps most startling is that the threat increases as our companies become more successful.

The villain? Human nature in the form of a couple of tendencies we just can't seem to get away from. First,

is the tendency we have to try to make decisions that everyone in our close working group will agree with.[4] And second, the biggest culprit—think of it as *Groupthink-on-Steroids*—

is the tendency we have to make decisions with which the "establishment" (the "experts" in our organizations or fields) will agree.

Together these behaviors weigh us down in "what everyone knows": crushing new ideas, stifling breakthroughs, and, yes, killing innovation before it even surfaces. And unfortunately, there is a wealth of evidence to suggest that both of these behaviors are nearly inevitable in organizations. *Groupthink* has been written about extensively, and chances are that if you've had a course in human resources, psychology, or organizational development you've run across the term before. The real question may be why, when we are so smart about it, we continue to engage in it. *ExpertThink* is a term I came up with after studying the impact of expertise on decision making and finding that Groupthink didn't quite address everything that was happening. The terms are tightly linked but different, and both are discussed at length in Chapters 2 and 3. The key point here though is that as hard as we might try to guard against them, they insidiously insert themselves into our organizations and wreak havoc—or at the very least thwart optimal performance.

• INNOVATION PHASES AND FILTERS •

Consider the way ideas become reality in most organizations. First there is typically a challenge or opportunity to be addressed. Then someone comes up with an idea for addressing it. A stage of development or fine-tuning typically follows (this can be very short or, in the case of some product or technology innovations, very long) in order to apply the idea. The final result? An innovation (Figure 1-3). An improvement versus the way things were before.

But getting from one side of this funnel to the other is obviously easier said than done. And one of the key places in which we get held up is the area between creative idea and application.

Think about your own company. If you were counseling new employees on how to present a new idea, what tips would you give them about how decisions are made? How would you suggest they position their ideas for greatest success? Maybe you'd advise them to pre-sell their idea to certain key people prior to a group meeting to assure that those influential decision makers would

Figure 1-3. Phases of innovation.

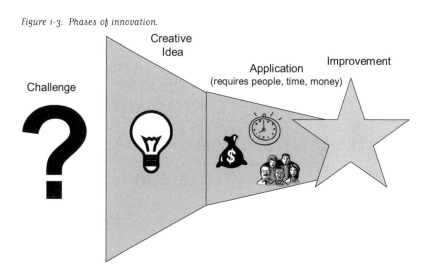

sway the conversation in favor of the new proposal. This was certainly a prerequisite for success in more than one group I've worked with.

Or maybe you'd tell them to introduce a new idea with facts and figures and reams of research to support their thinking—something other groups I've encountered required. You might even advise them on the best way to position an idea versus the status quo for maximum appeal.

Whatever you told them, you would be introducing them to the organizational filters through which all new ideas must pass. Even companies that on the surface seem to be wide open to new ways of thinking can have such stringent filters in place that few new ideas actually make it to implementation (they don't become innovations). Think of it this way: A funnel can be wide open at one end, but so narrow and specifically shaped on the other that only those ideas that fit the preconceived mold get through (Figures 1-4 and 1-5).

Where do these filters come from? Expertise. Both organizational and individual. Call them management filters, resource filters, whatever. In the end someone's experience determines whether resources are allocated to this battle or that one. The

Figure 1-4. Ideas must pass through filters.

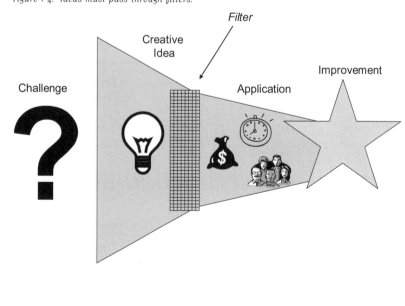

Figure 1-5. Filters can be too tight.

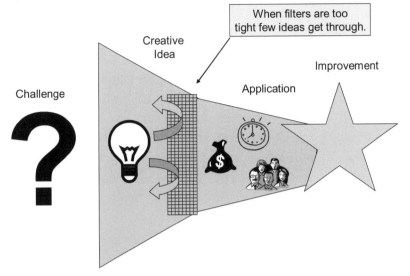

more successful and "expert" an organization is, the more filters it is likely to have in place. Clayton Christensen suggests in his book, *The Innovator's Dilemma*, that the very structures and processes we establish to support our businesses create "disabilities" for us in terms of disruptive innovation.[5] In other words, our filters help us get a little better at what we already do, but act as formidable barriers to doing something a whole lot better or even completely differently. What filters would you tell a new employee about at your company? What sort of ExpertThink do you deal with every day?

• THE AH-HAH! OF THE PERPETUAL NOVICE •

My fascination with the filters companies use to evaluate new ideas developed after leaving the customer products world and spending several years marketing and developing strategies for new products at Intel. Because I was not an engineer, it seemed that I was the perpetual novice. Certainly my business background and experience were valuable, but to truly add strategic insights when discussing a technology business, a certain level of understanding about the technology itself— as well as related technologies that it will displace, affect, or with which it will interact—is required. So, every new project I worked on started with an incredible ramp period in which I would attempt to soak in as much information as possible about the technology and then align it with what I knew about business.

One of the most important ways I learned during this ramp period was by talking with engineers. And this is where a big "ah-hah" came to me. As frustrating and time consuming as it was for some of my engineering counterparts to walk me through engineering 101, the exercise was frequently as valuable to them as it was to me.

> ▶As frustrating and time consuming as it was for some of my engineering counterparts to walk me through engineering 101, the exercise was frequently as valuable to them as it was to me. ■

As a result of my basic foundational questions and my annoying chorus of "why?—why?—why?" they were forced to think about the technology in ways they never had before. They sought new analogies. They restated. They struggled to make the difficult simple. And in the process, they and we often came up with ideas that were highly valuable and innovative—both from a technology and business standpoint.

Much as I might like to believe it, the skills I brought to these sessions were probably not all that exceptional. Nor do I believe that there was anything particularly unique about the engineering teams I worked with (except, of course that they were all composed of incredibly bright people).

Instead, there seemed to be something powerful about the process, and the mix of people. Deep domain experts (engineers in this case) were pushed out of their comfort zone. And a nonexpert (at least in engineering) was forced to link what she did know (in this case about business) with what she was just learning (about the technical challenge at hand). Deep Expertise + Expertise-in-a-Different-But-Related-Discipline seemed to be a formidable combination. Said another way, the prolonged presence of an outsider, who was not weighed down by the conventions of expertise, acted as a hyper-stimulant for creative ideas that could actually be implemented. Filters became less constrained. A different perspective suggested alternate paths. Innovative thinking flourished (Figure 1-6).

This book is the result of the research and real-life experiments I conducted to better understand what was taking place (and why) in those sessions and to determine whether it could be replicated in other types of organizations. I am not a professional researcher. I am a businessperson. So I relied on the wealth of research, analysis, and case studies that have been published in the fields of social psychology, innovation, creative thinking, organizational management, economics and a host of other areas. I also relied heavily on my personal experience and insights as well as those of respected colleagues in the business and academic communities.

Figure 1-6. Zero-Gravity Thinker can help team reconsider the filters.

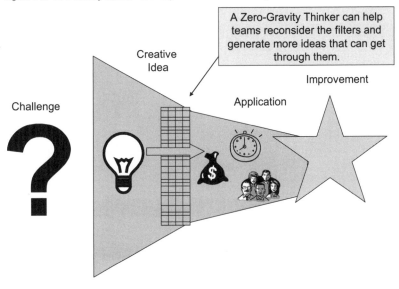

What I found supported many of the intuitive conclusions I had reached over the years about why it is often so difficult for successful people in successful organizations to think innovatively. More important, the findings also supported and expanded on the conclusions I had made regarding how to overcome the challenge. In particular, I found the work of Harvard Business School professor Dorothy Leonard and Tufts University professor Walter Swap in their book, *When Sparks Fly*,[6] quite insightful. This was one of the first "academic" sources I found to validate the concept of bringing "aliens" (complete outsiders) to teams as a way to stimulate innovative thinking. And, in fact, during the first year that I tested this concept at Intel, my role as a Zero-Gravity Thinker was actually referred to as one of an "embedded alien".

• TWO NOTES •

Finally, two notes are important. The first is that I offer the concept of Zero-Gravity Thinkers as work-in-progress. There is a significant amount of ever-growing research and anecdotal evidence from organizations using some version of the idea to establish a foundation for the approach. However, time and broader organizational use of the concept will undoubtedly add refinements.

The second note is that Zero-Gravity Thinkers aren't a magic solution. There is no cure-all for the stuck-in-the-mud organization. Long-term, successful innovation requires a deep commitment to fostering diversity of thought and action. The challenges are vast, spanning hiring practices, strategic direction, culture, management practices, and even the process of innovation. Implementing any one program or idea won't address everything. There are, unfortunately, many more books to read and lessons to be learned.

Having said this, Zero-Gravity Thinkers are a high-value tool. In particular, they can play a role in the very front end of the innovation process—when we should be most open to exploring a range of ideas and possibilities, but often aren't. They can help us re-align our filters by combating the Groupthink and ExpertThink that plague us. They can help us combine the power of the intuitive mind with the power of the expert mind. They can help us escape the weight of what we know (Figure 1-7).

Figure 1-7. Zero-Gravity-Thinker zone.

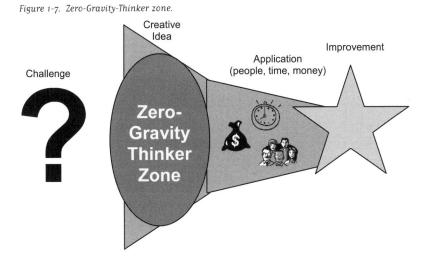

• KEY POINTS •

1. In this book innovation is defined as the application of an idea that results in a valuable improvement. No distinction is made between a radical or disruptive innovation and an incremental one.

2. Certain aspects of human nature inhibit innovation. In particular, people have a tendency to make decisions like the people with whom they work most closely. This is Groupthink. People also have a tendency to go along with the tried and true methods of experts. This is ExpertThink.

3. Zero-Gravity Thinkers are outsiders with specific characteristics (to be introduced later in the book) who, when immersed in a challenge with a team's experts, can help stimulate innovation by disrupting Groupthink and ExpertThink.

CHAPTER 2

GROUPTHINK: THE STRONGEST FORCE ON EARTH

WHY SUSTAINED INNOVATION IS SO DARNED HARD: PART 1

*Insanity in individuals is something rare—
but in groups, parties, nations, and epochs, it is
the rule. — Friedrich Nietzsche*

IN ORDER TO UNDERSTAND how "what we know"—and especially "what we collectively know"—can thwart innovation, it's helpful to first explore the way human nature frequently compels us to go along with the crowd.

Whether we want to admit it or not, we are dependent on other people for our well-being. Coworkers, bosses, members of our professional associations, etc., all can have an impact on how much money we make, what professional credentials we attain, even how much social status we have. As a result, there is a lot of evidence to suggest we're hard-wired to conform (sometimes at almost any cost) with the people we work with. But that's not usually a recipe for innovation. In fact "Innovation by Consensus" could be considered an oxymoron.

This chapter explores our tendency to Groupthink and focuses on how and why it continues to plague us. Note that many of the chapter's detailed examples of this behavior-in-action are government related. This is because government failures of huge magnitude are often painstakingly dissected and thus rich sources of data. Business leaders should not be distracted by this. The underlying factors that lead to Groupthink in a civic organization are the same as those that produce it in a for-profit entity. The opportunity is to understand and address those factors.

• NO ONE IS IMMUNE •

The term "Groupthink" was coined in 1972 by a Yale social psychologist named Irving Janis.[1] He used it to describe the tendency of people working in groups to try to reach unanimous decisions—even if those decisions aren't necessarily good ones.

Janis believed that Groupthink results in flawed decision making based on the fact that members of groups with the majority opinion tend to exert pressure on members with minority opinions to go along with the crowd. In other words, groups are not typically bastions of open-mindedness.

I'd take this one step further. I believe that Groupthink is one of the greatest threats to innovation that any organization faces. Trying to overcome this force is like trying to escape the pull of Earth's gravity. Our most basic instinct is simply not to fight it.

> ►Groupthink is one of the greatest threats to innovation that any organization faces. ■

The issue is that Groupthink turns otherwise brilliant, independent-minded people into herd animals. As difficult as it may be to believe, it happens to the best and brightest of us with alarming regularity. Take a look at the following two cases. The first is the landmark study Janis conducted regarding the Bay of Pigs fiasco in 1961. It illustrates the basic nature and dangers of Groupthink and was cited extensively in Janis's research. The second case centers on the more recent Enron collapse in 2001. In both cases a key takeaway is that even highly respected and successful individuals can be sucked into Groupthink behavior. Critically, note that there is a nearly forty-year time span between the two cases. Groupthink is tenacious. Even with all our management smarts it still haunts us.

CASE 1. BAY OF PIGS: GROUPTHINK AMONG THE BEST AND THE BRIGHTEST

The year was 1961. John F. Kennedy was President of the United States and had been given a plan by the CIA to invade Cuba and overthrow Fidel Castro. Kennedy liked the plan but wanted to hear what his advisors thought, and so he gathered them together.

During the course of a multi-hour discussion an interesting dynamic occurred. The people in the room who were aligned with Kennedy and liked the plan became louder and more aggressive in their defense of it. Conversely, the people who had reservations about the plan became quieter and more passive.

It is important to note that this wasn't a group of "yes men." These were high-profile, highly intelligent people, including Secretary of State Dean Rusk, Secretary of Defense Robert McNamara, Attorney General Robert Kennedy, and Arthur Schlesinger, Jr., presidential advisor and a noted Harvard historian. These men were noted for their integrity, intelligence, and willingness to voice their opinion. Nevertheless, by the end of the conversation, those who "dissented" from the majority and did not support the plan were so quiet that Kennedy believed he had a unanimous decision to move forward.

Of course, Bay of Pigs was a disaster. When Janis looked at what had gone wrong in the decision-making process he noted eight traits as hallmarks of Groupthink.

Hallmarks of Groupthink[2]

1. Conformity pressure on the minority
2. Self-censorship
3. Illusion of unanimity
4. Shared mind-set/stereotypes
5. Unquestioned belief in the inherent morality of the group
6. Collective rationalization of group's decisions
7. Illusion of invulnerability
8. Protection of the group from negative information

[*Note*: The above numbers are referenced in the paragraph below.]

In the Bay of Pigs example, every one of these Groupthink attributes was present. The majority exerted enormous pressure on the minority to conform to their point of view (1), and the minority reacted by increasingly censoring their opinions (2). In the end, this gave Kennedy and the majority the illusion of unanimity where none, in fact, existed (3).

In addition, the majority who favored the CIA's plan all had a shared mindset (4). Although they had no hard supporting evidence, these advisors believed that the citizens of Cuba wanted Fidel Castro to be overthrown. Apparently, they believed so strongly in the inherent morality of the U.S. efforts (5), that they were able to rationalize their decision to move forward as the only "virtuous" course of action (6). And, as the coup de grace, their feelings of moral superiority led them to feel a sense of invulnerability; as if the United States were already destined to win this battle (7).

Unfortunately, victory wasn't preordained. All members of the invasion force were either killed or captured. In part this was because the citizens of Cuba did not support the invasion and, in fact, took up arms against the invaders. Additionally, the advisors hadn't bothered to dig deeply enough into the CIA's plan to understand that the escape route for the invasion force was through an impassable swamp (8). Our forces were trapped—destined from the outset not to win, but to lose.[3]

Arthur Schlesinger later said, "In the months after the Bay of Pigs I bitterly reproached myself for having kept so silent during those crucial discussions in the Cabinet Room, though my feelings of guilt were tempered by the knowledge that a course of objection would have accomplished little save gain me a name as a nuisance. I can only explain my failure to do more than raise a few timid questions by reporting that one's impulse to blow the whistle on this nonsense was simply undone by the circumstances of the discussion."[4]

After studying this case, Janis figured that if such an elite group as Kennedy's advisors could be negatively affected by Groupthink, then the rest of us could too—and the last four decades have proven him right.

CASE 2. ENRON:
GROUPTHINK AMONG THE OVERSEERS

Every year from 1996 to 2000 Enron, an energy trading and communications firm, was named "America's Most Innovative Company" by *Fortune* Magazine. The company, based in Houston, Texas, had grown from $2 billion in market capitalization in 1985 to approximately $70 billion at its peak in 2000. This was largely the doing of Kenneth Lay, who was CEO from 1985 to early 2001, when he became chairman of the board and when Jeffrey Skilling assumed the role of CEO. Enron originally distributed electricity and gas throughout the United States and operated numerous power plants and pipelines worldwide. Under Lay's guidance, however, it pioneered new methods of trading power and even expanded into communications. These new trading methods made the company wealthy and gave it its reputation for innovative excellence. Unfortunately, the methods and the underlying accounting that supported them were largely illegal, resulting in the largest corporate failure in history.

One the most perplexing aspects of the Enron collapse is the role the board of directors played (or failed to play). In reviewing the board's role, the U.S. Senate's Permanent Subcommittee on Investigations concluded that "the Board saw but ignored numerous questionable practices by Enron management to the detriment of

Enron shareholders, employees, and business associates and contributed to the company's downfall."[5]

The report cites numerous failures of duty by the Board, including "the failure to stop Enron from using misleading accounting; the failure to protect Enron shareholders from unfair dealing in a partnership in which an Enron officer had a personal financial interest; the failure to ensure adequate public disclosure of material off-the-books liabilities; the failure to ensure the independence of the company's auditor, Arthur Andersen; and the failure to monitor or halt abuse by Enron's board chairman and chief executive officer Kenneth Lay of a company-financed, multi-million dollar, personal credit line."[6]

The big question is why? Reports by the Senate and others since Enron's collapse have been scathing in their criticism of Enron's board. But, there is no evidence that its actions (or inaction) were based on greed or the promise of personal gain.

The members of the board were highly respected leaders in a variety of world-class businesses and organizations. None of them had built their careers by being shrinking violets. Yet once in Enron's boardroom, shrinking violets is what they seem to have become. A March 1, 2004 article in the *New Yorker* noted that while the directors were all undisputed leaders in their own organizations, when brought together, "they turned into meek conformists."[7]

I'll state what many believe to be obvious. Groupthink was a primary culprit. This board of directors had one objective: to protect the interests of shareholders. But, perhaps lulled into a sense of invulnerability or a feeling of superiority based on the success of Enron, they failed in that mission. Maybe they all simply wanted to get along. Then again, maybe they simply started to believe their own press. After all, in 2000 (one year before Enron's collapse) *CEO Magazine* named Enron's board one of the top five boards of the year.

Groupthink in a Test Tube

As the previous two cases illustrate, Groupthink doesn't discriminate. It is not necessarily the result of a weak personality or low self-esteem. Although Janis believed that some people were more susceptible than others to "going along with the group," he be-

Enron Board Members as Listed in the
2000 Enron Annual Report

Robert A. Belfer
Chairman, Belco Oil & Gas Corp.

Norman P. Blake, Jr.
Chairman, president, and CEO,
Comdisco, Inc.
and former CEO and secretary
general, United States Olympic
Committee

Ronnie C. Chan
Chairman, Hang Lung Group

John H. Duncan
Former chairman of the executive
committee of Gulf & Western
Industries, Inc.

Wendy L. Gramm
Director of the Regulatory Studies
Program of the Mercatus Center at
George Mason University
and former chairman, U.S. Commodity
Futures Trading Commission

Ken L. Harrison
Former chairman and CEO, Portland
General Electric Company

Robert K. Jaedicke
Professor of Accounting (Emeritus)
and former dean, Graduate School of
Business, Stanford University

Kenneth L. Lay
Chairman, Enron Corp.

Charles A. Lemaistre
President emeritus, University of
Texas M.D. Anderson Cancer Center

John Mendelsohn
President, University of Texas M.D.
Anderson Cancer Center

Jerome J. Meyer
Chairman, Tektronix, Inc.

Paulo V. Ferraz Pereira
Executive vice president of Group
Bozano
Former president and COO, Meridional
Financial Group
and former president and CEO, State
Bank of Rio De Janeiro, Brazil

Frank Savage
Chairman, Alliance Capital
Management International

Jeffrey K. Skilling
President and CEO, Enron Corp.

John A. Urquhart
Senior advisor to the chairman, Enron
Corp.
President, John A. Urquhart Associates
and former senior vice president of
Industrial and Power Systems, General
Electric Company

John Wakeham
Former U.K. Secretary of State for
Energy and leader of the Houses of
Lords and Commons

Herbert S. Winokur, Jr.
President, Winokur Holdings, Inc.
and former senior executive vice
president, Penn Central Corporation

lieved that given the right circumstances no one was immune. In the Bay of Pigs and the Enron board examples, highly intelligent and independent-minded people fell victim, perhaps in part because they valued the collegial nature of the relationship with their cohorts. But what about groups of strangers? If a person has no long-term vested interest in what others think of him, how persuasive can "the group" be in his decision making? Turns out . . . pretty persuasive.

In 1958 social psychologist Solomon Asch sought to find out how much of an impact groups could wield. In his study, college students in groups of eight to ten were shown two cards (Figure 2-1). The first card contained a single line. The students were told that the study was on visual perception and were then asked to identify which of the three lines on the second card, labeled A, B, and C, was the same length as the single line on the "test" card.

The twist in this study was that only one of the participants in each group was actually being "tested." The other participants were all working with the scientist and were given preprogrammed responses to the questions Asch posed.

In the experiments various numbers of participants who were in on the scheme were told to give an incorrect answer, saying for instance that line A (see Figure 2-1) was the same length as the

Figure 2-1. Solomon Asch's group conformity experiment.

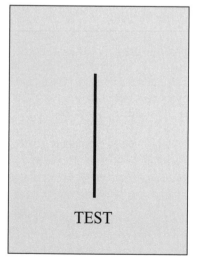

single line on the test card. Sometimes all of the fake participants would give the same wrong answer. Other times some would give false answers while the rest answered correctly. What was startling was that even when the majority was obviously wrong, the test subjects went along with them in about 33 percent of the experiments. And over the course of several experiments, 74 percent of the subjects went along with an erroneous majority group at least once. This puts a whole new spin on majority rules, doesn't it? Asch, who had initially been trying to disprove that individuals would yield to the will of the group, was disturbed by his findings and stated:

> The tendency to conformity in our society is so strong that reasonably intelligent and well-meaning young people are willing to call white black. This is a matter of concern. It raises questions about our ways of education and about the values that guide our conduct."[8]

Altered Reality

Far more disturbing is the experiment conducted at Stanford University in 1971 by Philip Zimbardo, a psychology Ph.D. In this study a group of young men who had tested as very "normal" volunteered to participate in a situation simulating prison conditions. Half of the young men were arbitrarily assigned the role of guards. The other half were assigned the role of prisoners.

It seems that the environment these young men were placed in, along with the roles they were asked to play, began to feel all too real. What would normally have been considered cruel and sadistic behavior by the participants who played the guards (depriving "prisoners" of food or sleep or bathroom access) became the accepted "norm" in the mock prison environment. The "guards'" use of these behaviors as control weapons escalated in such a disturbing manner over the course of just a few days that a couple of the "prisoners" had emotional breakdowns and had to be excused from the program before the experiment was stopped completely.

As Zimbardo wrote, "We had to call off the experiment and close down our prison after only six days of what might have been a two-week long study of the psychological dynamics of prison life. We had to do so because too many normal young men were behaving pathologically as powerless prisoners or as sadistic, all-powerful guards"[9]

The important thing to note here is that this behavior wasn't forced on any of the participants by an authority figure. An ordinary peer group of young men talked one another into engaging in actions that none would normally have considered themselves capable of. In other words, all of these people simply went along with the group.

There are striking similarities between this experiment and the actual abuses that took place in Abu Ghraib prison in Iraq in 2004. Shortly after the U.S. invasion, the notorious Abu Ghraib facility, where Saddam Hussein was believed to have ordered the torture of thousands, was converted into a U.S. military prison. Military police with no formal training in prison operations were assigned to run the facility.

There is much debate about whether the abuses that took place in 2003 and 2004 were the result of "orders" from military police or other officials in the military chain of command, or the result of a peer group "gone bad." In either case, Princeton professor Susan Fiske, author of the article "Why Ordinary People Torture Enemy Prisoners,"[10] contends that peer pressure, pressure from authority figures, and even situations can influence behavior in uncharacteristic ways. "Could any average 18-year-old have tortured these prisoners? I would have to answer, 'Yes, just about anyone could have,'" Fiske says.[11]

• BUT WE'RE SMARTER THAN THAT •

But, you may ask, what happens when organizations are "smart" about Groupthink and group dynamics? Certainly if managers and employees are educated, they can put safeguards in place to prevent poor decision making and innovation-squelching behavior, right? Evidence suggests this might not always be true. Take a look at the following two cases about NASA's shuttle disasters and the CIA's faulty intelligence on weapons of mass destruction in Iraq.

CASE 3. NASA'S SHUTTLE DISASTERS: RECURRING GROUPTHINK

Many of us remember all too well exactly where we were and what we were doing when we heard of the Challenger shuttle explosion on January 28, 1986 (Figure 2-2).

Figure 2-2. *Explosion of space shuttle Challenger.* Photo courtesy of National Aeronautics and Space Administration.

I remember hearing the news at work and sitting in disbelief at my desk. The explosion killed all seven astronauts aboard, including the high school teacher, Christa McAuliffe, who had planned to teach America's schoolchildren a lesson from space. It also sent NASA into a tailspin, blowing the lid off of the close-minded, protectionist atmosphere that had evolved in that institution.

The sad fact is that the Challenger disaster might have been prevented. As many of you may remember, Roger Boisjoly, an engineer working on the Challenger mission, began warning of a significant issue with the O-rings on the shuttle a year before the fatal catastrophe. The O-rings connected segments of the solid rocket booster, which was used to bring the shuttle into orbit. Boisjoly worked for Morton Thiokol, the O-ring manufacturer, and had noted as early as January 1985 that the O-rings did not function properly in cold weather.

Throughout 1985, Boisjoly pushed Morton Thiokol and NASA to work urgently to resolve the issue. Following is an excerpt from a memo he wrote to the vice president of engineering at Morton Thiokol on July 31, 1985—six months prior to the disaster:

> It is my honest and very real fear that if we do not take immediate action to dedicate a team to solve the problem with the field joint having the number one priority, then we stand in

jeopardy of losing a flight along with all the launch pad facilities."[12]

During that year Boisjoly's efforts met with a lukewarm response. In fact, he was asked to downplay his concerns. In his U.S. Senate testimony regarding a presentation he gave to 130 technical experts at a conference of the Society of Automotive Engineers in October 1985 (three months prior to the Challenger disaster) regarding O-rings and other "joints" on the shuttle, Boisjoly said:

> I was given strict instructions, which came from MSFC [NASA's Marshall Space Flight Center], not to express the critical urgency of fixing the joint but to only emphasize the joint improvement aspect during my presentation."[13]

Armed with research data and considerable evidence to support the case, Boisjoly went so far as to try to stop the launch the day before it took place. In hindsight it seems incredible that NASA and Morton Thiokol wouldn't have listened more closely to him. But Groupthink is a powerful force.

NASA managers were facing extreme economic and political pressure to launch the Challenger on schedule. Where there was opportunity to doubt the conclusions of a handful of people on the contractor's engineering staff (when NASA's own staff considered the mission a "go") their circumstances made them inclined to do so. Couple this with the fact that numerous shuttle missions had already been flown with the "faulty" O-rings, and NASA's thought process becomes even clearer. Because nothing bad had happened so far, they assumed nothing bad would happen in the future. Reminds you of the way a loser in Russian Roulette might think, doesn't it?

In the end, confident that they had designed the "perfect" shuttle, NASA managers exerted pressure on Morton Thiokol managers to clear the launch. In turn, Morton Thiokol decided to disregard the minority opinion presented by Boisjoly that the mission was in jeopardy. Majority ruled with devastating consequences.

CASE 3.5.
NASA GROUPTHINK REDUX

You would think that after Challenger, NASA's culture would have changed. Unfortunately this doesn't seem to have been the case. On

February 1, 2003—seventeen years after the Challenger disaster—the space shuttle Columbia was lost as it re-entered the Earth's atmosphere. Although the mechanical reasons for the disaster were different, the errors in management and decision making were strikingly similar. Engineers had known for some time that the heat shields on the wings might be vulnerable. They failed, however, to bring this to the attention of senior NASA management. Even after the shuttle had been struck by debris during launch (potentially damaging the heat shield), little was done by the engineering team or NASA management (such as, for example, reviewing pictures of the damage) to verify that the impact had NOT put the mission in jeopardy. Success was simply assumed. According to Charles L. Bosk, a sociology professor at the University of Pennsylvania who teaches a class on NASA, "Engineers were forced to pass an answer, not confusion and uncertainty, up to the next level and they appeared to be heavily influenced by the agency's "can-do" atmosphere. That's really chilling—the notion that failure . . . is not an option."[14]

In August 2003, the Columbia Accident Investigation Board issued a scathing report, blaming a lack of leadership and open-mindedness in management for the disaster. It specifically noted NASA's failure to learn from the Challenger disaster nearly two decades before as a key factor in the Columbia accident. According to the report:

> In the aftermath of the Challenger accident . . . there was a resistance to externally imposed changes and an attempt to maintain the internal belief that NASA was still a "perfect place" alone in its ability to execute a program of human space flight. . . . Managers lost their ability to accept criticism, leading them to reject the recommendations of many boards and blue ribbon panels, the Rogers Commission (Presidential Commission on the Space Shuttle Challenger) among them."[15]

Once a culture of Groupthink sets in, it can be nearly impossible to dislodge, though NASA's successful launch and return of the space shuttle Discovery in the summer of 2005 lends hope for this venerable institution. History seems to show, however, that even in organizations that have safeguards in place against Groupthink, it can sneak in anyway, as in this final case.

"Group Think" Backed Prewar Assumptions
New York Times, July 10, 2004

Regardless of what you think of the war in Iraq, the reason given by the U.S. government for invading that country in 2004 was that Iraq possessed weapons of mass destruction (WMDs). This intelligence came from the CIA and, embarrassingly, was wrong.

When WMDs had yet to be found in Iraq months after the U.S. invasion, a special Senate panel was formed to evaluate the CIA's intelligence. The resulting 512-page report lambasted the CIA for a culture of groupthink that led to the faulty WMD assumptions.

According to the report, the root of the mindset about WMDs dated back to the 1990/91 Gulf War with Iraq. Evidence of Iraq's WMD program discovered at that time caught the Intelligence Community (IC) off-guard. Although Iraq agreed to discontinue the program following the war, the IC retained the belief that Iraq would re-engage the program if given the opportunity.

When UN weapons inspectors left the country in 1998, the CIA assumed the worst and evaluated all information it received with that notion in mind. The Senate report states that "the IC had a tendency to accept information which supported the presumption that Iraq had active and expanded WMD programs. . . . Information that contradicted the IC's presumption . . . was often ignored."

This behavior continued even after UN weapons inspectors returned to Iraq in November of 2002. The CIA routinely rejected information from those inspectors that contradicted the notion that Iraq had reinstated its WMD program. IC analysts were so convinced that Iraq was deceiving the world that they mentally discarded information that suggested otherwise.

Apparently, the CIA didn't think anyone else should be influenced by dissenting information either. The intelligence the CIA supplied to U.S. government leaders that ultimately resulted in the decision to go to war did not include information from agencies that disagreed with the findings. The Senate investigation document states that the CIA's pre-war intelligence reports "provided readers with an incomplete picture of the nature and extent of the debate within the Intelligence Community regarding these issues."

Further, the CIA's carefully worded document also eliminated clarifiers that would have given readers a better sense of the "judgment" nature of the analysis. According to the Senate panel's report, "Removing caveats such as 'we judge' and 'we assess' changed many sentences in the unclassified paper to statements of fact rather than assessments."

The Senate report states "IC personnel involved in the Iraq WMD issue demonstrated several aspects of groupthink:

➤ Examining few alternatives
➤ Selective gathering of information
➤ Pressure to conform within the group or withhold criticism
➤ Collective rationalization"

What is interesting is that the CIA is well versed in the dangers of groupthink. In fact, they regularly employ various methods to help guard against it. A 1999 report published by the CIA's Center for the Study of Intelligence highlights the following actions managers should take in order to establish the optimal environment for the analysis of intelligence. In particular, note that the third and fourth bullets are directly targeted to disrupt Groupthink.

CIA Anti-Groupthink Guidelines (paraphrased)

1. Support research that will improve the understanding of how decisions are made.
2. Train analysts in thinking and analysis skills that will enhance their judgments.
3. Expose analysts to alternative mindsets to help them evaluate information from multiple perspectives.
4. Make sure that the possible but unlikely scenario is analyzed along with the most likely scenario to assure all potential outcomes are adequately considered.[16]

Unfortunately, perhaps anxious not to miss another 9/11 type threat, the CIA seemed to have put its own recommendations aside where the question of Iraqi WMDs was concerned.

• SO WHAT? •

You may look at these high-profile examples from government and boards of directors and wonder what they have to do with your business. After all, most management mistakes don't result in such spectacular failures. But between 2000 and 2003 there were over 149,000 companies in the United States that filed for bankruptcy protection.[17] I wonder what role selective information-gathering, collective rationalization, or just the plain old close-mindedness of Groupthink might have played in these less publicized (but to the people involved, just as excruciating) downfalls?

Before you decide whether Groupthink might be affecting your business, ask yourself whether you can think of a time in the past year when you have been less aggressive in stating your opinion, or less vocal in outlining your point of view than you otherwise might have been, BECAUSE you knew your opinion was at odds with that of the rest of the group you work with.

In speeches I've given on this topic, 95 percent of the audience typically raises their hands in response to this question. In honesty, I have to wonder whether the other 5 percent are still employed. Most people learn before kindergarten that sometimes you just have to keep your mouth shut. And maybe that's why Groupthink is so tough to overcome. The behavior that spawns it is self-preserving from an individual standpoint. It's only lethal to the collective.

> Alfred Sloan, who ran General Motors from 1923 to 1956, was onto something when he said at a meeting, "Gentlemen, I take it that we are all in complete agreement on the decision here. Then, I propose that we postpone further discussion . . . to give ourselves time to develop disagreement and perhaps gain some understanding of what the decision is all about."[18] ■

• KEY POINTS •

1. Groupthink is a well-documented and often detrimental human tendency to go along with decisions that the majority of a group will accept. Although there is high awareness of the concept, it continues to plague organizations.

2. No one is immune from groupthink. The most seasoned leaders and the most junior followers have been victims.

3. Even our best efforts to guard against it sometimes fail. To battle groupthink is to battle human nature.

CHAPTER 3

· · · · · · · · · · · · · · · · · ·

EXPERTTHINK: GROUPTHINK ON STEROIDS

WHY SUSTAINED INNOVATION IS SO DARNED HARD: PART 2

When everybody knows that something is so, it means that nobody knows nothin'. — *Attributed to Alois Xavier Schmidt, professor at the City College of New York, by Andy Grove when asked about the best advice he ever received.*[1]

GROUPTHINK IS ABOUT GOING ALONG <u>to get</u> <u>along. ExpertThink is about going along to get ahead</u>—or at least not get left behind. It's an overzealous inclination we have to align with the boss, with best-known methods, even with what we have been taught about "the way things are" in an effort to address challenges and opportunities as effectively as possible. Referring back to the Paradox of Expertise outlined in the Introduction to this book, there is a delicate balance between relying on the force of what we know to keep us from drifting aimlessly into space and allowing ourselves to be crushed by it. ExpertThink upsets that balance. Think of it this way. If Groupthink is like Earth's gravity, ExpertThink is like the force of a black hole—where not even light gets out.

But, we're getting ahead of ourselves. In order to explore ExpertThink we first need to take a look at the nature of expertise.

> ▶ If Groupthink is like Earth's gravity, ExpertThink is like
> the force of a black hole—where not even light gets
> out. ■

• EXPERTISE: THE PROS AND THE CONS •

The slightly musty-smelling, dog-eared 1960 edition of *Webster's New World Dictionary* that sits on my bookshelf says that an expert is one who is "very skillful; having much training and knowledge in some special field." A quick look at several newer online definitions indicates not much has changed in the last forty-five years. So, let's use this as our definition.

Let's also acknowledge that expertise is a valuable commodity. A defense attorney who has successfully tried numerous murder cases accumulates knowledge about the dos and don'ts associated with such trials. After a while that attorney is likely to have "seen it all" . . . or at least seen an awful lot. When new challenges arise, chances are they frequently look a lot like old challenges.

That's when expertise kicks in. Based on her skill, training, and knowledge, the defender is likely to respond quickly and with authority to familiar circumstances. This almost auto-response typically increases her efficiency and effectiveness. Over time, her expertise (along with a good track record for acquittals) is a valuable and sought-after commodity.

In philosophical terms, choosing the most familiar path or the simplest explanation (the short-cut) is known as *Occam's Razor*. Named for William of Occam, the 14th-century English Franciscan friar and philosopher who defined the concept, Occam's Razor states that when there are multiple possible explanations for a phenomenon, the simplest one is usually correct. And, the simplest explanation for a situation or solution to a problem is typically the one that looks like ones we've seen before.

Following Occam's Razor, our attorney-friend might very well believe, based on years of previous experience, that regardless of what her clients might claim, the simplest explanation is that every client is guilty. This may seem like a far-fetched example, but according to an article published in the American Bar Association's *Criminal Justice* Magazine, "more than 90 percent of criminal cases end in guilty pleas" and "many defense counsel work in a culture that tends to assume rather than question a defendant's guilt."[2]

The assumption of guilt impacts how our star defense attorney chooses to direct her attention and counsel her clients. Plea bargains are generally good; private detectives in search of the "real killer" are generally a waste of time.

But what happens when the simplest, most likely answer isn't the best one? What happens when expert judgment narrows thinking too much too soon? In the same issue of *Criminal Justice* Magazine, Ronald Huff, a professor in the Department of Criminology, Law and Society at the University of California, Irvine estimates that .5 percent (1/2 of 1 percent) of all criminal convictions in the United States each year are wrongful.[3] Though this may seem like a very small number, it represented over 7,500 cases in the year 2000. Imagine, 7,500 people punished for crimes they didn't commit, in part because their attorney's experience was working against them.

Allan W. Snyder, the foundation director of the Centre for the Mind at Australian National University says, "We become 'expert' when we can react automatically to things that are very important in our environment. Mental paradigms (mindsets) make possible this automatic behavior."[4] In fact, he says, mindsets are essential. They provide us with a frame of reference for everything in our

> ▶Imagine, 7,500 people punished for crimes they didn't commit, in part because their attorney's experience was working against them. ■

lives. They help us see patterns, recognize symbols, and distinguish important from unimportant details.

Here's a simplistic example. Imagine you are looking for a pen you dropped in a room that is semi-dark. You see three objects across the room: a water hose, a paintbrush, and a flashlight. Your mindset tells you that the object that is likely to be most helpful to you in finding your pen is the flashlight. You know this because you've used flashlights before. You know they emit light. And you know that the water hose and paintbrush don't. So you walk to it, turn it on and spot the missing pen on the floor.

But imagine you had no mindset at all, something that Professor Snyder likens to having some forms of autism. Without a mindset you have no way of drawing associations between objects and their uses or symbols and their meanings. You might need to test the water hose and the paintbrush before deciding to use the flashlight to help in your search. At their most basic, mindsets help us live our lives without reinventing the wheel over and again.

Of course there is a catch, and this is where expertise becomes dangerous to innovation. As Professor Snyder goes on to say, "The price for mindsets is fixed modes of thought and hence prejudice. Experts, in particular, appear to have extreme difficulty in questioning the foundations for their belief."[5]

Think about a task like driving, which after years of practice many of us feel proficient, if not expert at. If we turn the steering wheel to the left, we know the car will turn left. And if we apply simultaneous pressure to the brake we know we will accomplish a

> "Experts, in particular, appear to have extreme difficulty in questioning the foundations for their belief."—Allan Snyder ■

turn without sending the car into a ditch. We don't have to think so much as just do.

Now, imagine driving on snow and ice. Most of us (especially on the West Coast of the United States) don't have a firm mindset for this. It certainly wasn't automatic for me to turn the steering wheel left into a spin a few years ago during a snowstorm when all I really wanted to do was go straight. And, it also wasn't in my mindset to gently pump the brakes (before the anti-lock variety made this unnecessary) when my instinct was to slam on them.

In her book, *The Challenger Launch Decision,* Boston College sociologist Diane Vaughn writes that people are very reluctant to part with their mental models. "They may puzzle over contradictory evidence," she writes, "but usually succeed in pushing it aside—until they come across a piece of evidence too fascinating to ignore, too clear to misperceive, too painful to deny, which makes vivid still other signals they do not want to see, forcing them to alter and surrender the world-view they have so meticulously constructed."[6] Coming close to skidding into a ditch was enough evidence for me to change my driving habits in snow!

If you doubt that your own mindset is difficult to break, try a little experiment (you don't even have to leave your chair). Cross your arms. Now cross them the opposite way with your other arm on top. Hard isn't it? Most people have a preference for which arm goes where, and it's uncomfortable to try to change that. One man sheepishly admitted to me that he couldn't cross his arms the other way without really thinking about it. Though you might call this a physical mindset, mental mindsets can be just as difficult to change.

The point is that we often run on automatic pilot, using previously established and familiar patterns or those of the experts around us as our guide. This is particularly true when we're tired or in a hurry. And, when was the last time you weren't pressed for time at work?

• EXPERTTHINK: EXPERTISE GONE AWRY •

ExpertThink is the tendency of people in the same organizations, professions, or industries to start making decisions, analyzing situations, and evaluating ideas as if they all have the same mental mindset. Do you doubt that this can happen in enlightened companies with diverse workforces? I don't. Knowing what we know about Groupthink and expertise, I question how it could fail to happen.

Consider the consequences in a good organization when someone is successful at a key task. Perhaps a plant manager has found a way to reduce manufacturing costs, or a product manager has discovered the best way to position the company's key product for optimal sales. Smart organizations proliferate these learnings as quickly and efficiently as they can throughout the workforce. They set up systems for capturing and disseminating insights and information. They may even establish formal training programs. Over time most employees are exposed to and have adopted BKMs (best-known methods) in everything from product development to new employee hiring practices. In large part this shared mindset is key to the company's continued success. Everyone speaks the same language. Everyone stays focused on executing what works and avoiding what doesn't. Organizational expertise has been established.

Unfortunately, this is also when the organization becomes vulnerable to ExpertThink because the very practices meant to help an organization thrive make new or different ideas seem alien and unwelcome. In effect, organizational expertise can trigger a sort of immune response that kills "foreign" ideas as efficiently as the human immune system kills foreign substances—even when those ideas, like organ transplants in the human body, might be beneficial.

Perhaps most disturbing is that ExpertThink is powerful—far more powerful than Groupthink. In fact, ExpertThink is "Groupthink-on-Steroids." Where Groupthink typically occurs only in tight-knit teams, ExpertThink extends far beyond the immediate group. Senior experts or authorities don't even have to be present in a group discussion to exert their influence—the team is already well steeped in the "best" way to approach most issues.

►ExpertThink is Groupthink-on-Steroids. ■

I once worked with a company where the tentacles of Expert-Think were so far-reaching and powerful that even health risks couldn't counter them. The company made chemicals for use in agriculture. Most of its senior executives were in their forties or fifties and had been with the company or in the industry their entire careers. These senior managers took great pride in their products and product knowledge. In fact, they were so certain of their own "expertise" regarding the safety of a particular pesticide that in individual discussions I had with several of them, they scoffed at a new warning from the FDA that classified the primary chemical in their product as a carcinogen. A couple went so far as to brag about their continued use of the product in their own gardening without gloves! This attitude eventually permeated the organization and junior employees began voicing the same point of view . . . even when they weren't in the presence of senior company executives. Organizational ExpertThink was so strong in this company that not even the overriding expertise of an entity like the FDA could overcome it. At the very least, I hope these folks eventually conceded that donning a pair of gloves wasn't tantamount to company betrayal.

• FOLLOW THE LEADER •

Obviously ExpertThink is related to Groupthink in that it stems in part from a desire to go along with the opinions of people in the "establishment"—if not in our immediate workgroup. But, isn't alignment with the establishment another way of being aligned with authority?

Definitely. As I was researching this subject, I was surprised at how authority-driven we humans really are. Naively, I thought we had moved past those days into an era that celebrates the rugged individualist and sometimes even rewards the whistle-blower. Just look around. Popular Western culture (particularly American culture) oozes an anti-authority message. Take movies for instance. From *Dr. Doolittle* to *The Matrix* to *Miss Congeniality,* many have a common theme: Don't go along with the crowd; don't take the

*Figure 3-1. The New Yorker Collection, 1994, Mick Stevens from cartoonbank.com. *

"I don't know how it started, either. All I know is that it's part of our corporate culture."

easy way out; trust yourself, not the group or, heaven forbid, some authority figure. Everyone after all, loves a cowboy.

But for all of our idolization of the individual, we sure go along with the boss a lot. In a study published in the *California Management Review* last year, it was noted that seven out of ten employees in American businesses say they don't speak up when their opinions are at odds with their superiors. Seventy percent! Even when we KNOW we are right, most of us don't say anything![7]

"Captainitis" is the term an article published in the *Harvard Management Communication Letter* used to describe the tendency people have not to question authority. The name comes from the disastrous accidents that have occurred on flights with multiple crew members when a senior crew member makes a mistake that no one else corrects.

The article quotes an exchange between pilot and copilot, as captured on the flight recorder before the plane plunged into the Potomac River near Washington, D.C. in 1982.

Copilot: "Let's check the ice on those tops (wings) again since we've been sitting here a while."

Captain: "No. I think we get to go in a minute."

Copilot: (Referring to an instrument reading) "Uh, that doesn't seem right, does it? Uh, that's not right."

Captain: "Yes, it is."

Copilot: "Uh, maybe it is . . . "

(Sound of plane straining unsuccessfully to gain altitude)

Copilot: "Larry, we're going down."

Captain: "I know it."

(Sound of impact that killed the captain, copilot, and seventy-six others on board) [8]

How much sage advice is being withheld from us? How many good ideas (or warnings) are we missing out on? How many are we keeping to ourselves?

A famous (or some would say infamous) experiment by Stanley Milgram, a U.S. social psychologist, showed just how far we would go to align with authority. Milgram brought together a group of presumably normal people and told them they were participating in an experiment dealing with the relationship between punishment and learning. One of the experimenters, the person in authority, instructed the participants to shock a learner by pressing a lever on a machine each time the learner made a mistake in a word-matching task. Each subsequent shock was stronger than the last, with the starting voltage at 15 volts (painful) and the top voltage at 450 volts (very painful and potentially lethal).[9]

In actuality, the shock machine was a prop and the "learner" was an actor who did not actually get shocked, but made a lot of noise as if he were. The participants did not know this until after the experiment was over, however. The result? Sixty-five percent of participants, all deemed to be "normal people," continued to obey the instructions of the "experimenter" to the very end—delivering what they believed to be a potentially fatal 450 volt shock even as they heard their "student" screaming.

Milgram's study met with a sort of morbid fascination, and although many questioned the findings, other studies have since replicated the results. Hard as it may be for many of us to believe, it seems that when instructed by a person of "authority" in an environment where the actions are deemed "acceptable," most human beings will act in a way that would otherwise be entirely out of character. In Milgram's experiment people knowingly inflicted what they believed to be severe and potentially fatal pain on others just because they were told to!

• CATCH-22 •

As already noted, experts in an organization don't even have to be present in a discussion to exert influence, but what happens when they are? The likelihood of ExpertThink is multiplied!

Consider the study conducted by Leonard Karakowsky and Kenneth McBey of York University,[10] which confirms what we already intuitively know. According to their research, people who are recognized as having high levels of expertise and credibility participate much more vocally and aggressively in meetings than do other people. Further, when they do suggest ideas that differ from the majority, the group is more likely to listen.

It turns out that the punishing behavior associated with Groupthink is directed far more often at peers or at people who are perceived as having less expertise and credibility.[11] For most organizations this means that employees are most likely to listen to senior, revered managers and least likely to listen to new hires or the quiet guy who always seems to have ideas out in left field.

It's a real Catch 22. Employees are most likely to listen to the people who may be least likely to help the company innovate. I want to be clear that I'm not expert-bashing—we need expertise to progress. I'm also not suggesting that experts don't come up with innovative ideas. Of course they do. But evidence suggests we might want to reprioritize to whom we listen when innovation is the goal.

Take the case of Nikola Tesla for instance. Among other things, Tesla discovered the rotating magnetic field that is the basis of AC (alternating-current) machinery. Tesla was a student at the Joanneum Polytechnic School in Graz, Austria in 1876 and 1877. One day as he watched one of his professors, Jacob Poeschl, attempt to control the sparking of a DC (direct-current) motor—which was state-of-the-art at the time—Tesla suggested that it might be possible to build the motor in an entirely different manner, which would prevent sparking. The professor was irritated by the impudence of a mere student. Poeschl went so far as to lecture on the impossibility of creating such a motor and said, "Mr. Tesla may accomplish great things, but he certainly never will do this."

But even in the face of such authoritative scorn Tesla continued to ponder the possibilities until he had an epiphany. By breaking with convention completely, he conceived of a way to alter magnetic fields that did indeed eliminate sparking in motors. This breakthrough became the basis for the AC technology that enabled electricity to be transmitted across long distances and is the foundation of North America's power-grid system today.[12]

Going along with the crowd and with all of the "expert wisdom" that surrounds us can be expensive. To mention just a couple of examples we've talked about, the Enron collapse cost investors $25 billion[13] as well as undermined American confidence in corporate ethics. The Challenger disaster is estimated to have cost as much as $12 billion,[14] taking into account the cost of the Challenger itself, its replacement (Endeavor), and the clean-up and investigation. (It's impossible, of course, to put a dollar figure on the loss of human life resulting from the explosion.)

But downside cost is just one part of the equation. What about lost upside? Here's an excerpt from a speech I gave on how an entire industry lost out because it wouldn't listen to someone who wasn't an "expert" in their business.

▶Marion Donovan and the Greatest Invention of All Time

Let's bring all of this talk about ExpertThink and innovation close to home. Have you ever changed a baby's diaper? Have you ever used a cloth diaper? Was it a good experience for you?

It wasn't for me. The sum total of my experience with cloth diapers was one day. When my daughter was born my husband and I decided to get a diaper service and try cloth. At the time we thought we were being environmentally sensitive. (I won't go into that whole debate here.) But, what a mess! My daughter's clothes kept getting soaked. The bedding kept getting soaked. I must have done three weeks worth of laundry because I used cloth diapers for one day. My apologies to any cloth diaper manufacturers but based on that experience, I am tempted to say that the disposable diaper is, perhaps, the greatest innovation of all time. I think I would have gone without electricity rather than give up disposable diapers until my daughter was potty-trained!

Sadly, ExpertThink kept disposable diapers out of the hands of mainstream parents during the *entire decade* of the 1950s. Not only did those parents have to deal with the horrors of cloth diapers, but because of this behavior a number of companies who could have ridden the wave of a successful new product category completely missed the opportunity.

Marion Donovan's story is one of *a mother being the* mother of invention out of necessity. In 1946, disgusted that there was no diaper product that her infant

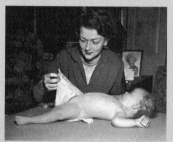

Figure 3-2. Marion O'Brien Donovan and "the greatest invention of all time." Marion O'Brien Donovan Papers, Archives Center, National Museum of American History, Smithsonian Institution.

daughter didn't wet through, Marion developed one herself. She called the initial version, made using nylon parachute cloth, the "boater" because it helped babies "stay afloat." Within a couple of years, Marion had upgraded her design to become the first paper diaper (Figure 3-2). She was granted a patent in 1951.

Subsequently, she tried to sell her invention to major baby product manufacturers. In a Barbara Walters interview in 1975 she said, "I went to all the big names that you can think of, and they said 'We don't want it. No woman has asked us for that. They're very happy and they buy all our baby pants.'" She was encouraged by the executives in these companies to go back home and leave the baby product development to the "experts."

So, while those 1950s parents were suffering through cloth diapers, Marion's invention sat for nearly ten years until, in 1960, a man named Victor Mills

bought her patent and invented Pampers. ■

I bet that a few of the executives Marion met with initially were disappointed they had dismissed this outsider's wild idea when Pampers hit the streets. As of 2003, the U.S. market alone for disposable diapers was $4 billion![15]

• THE ANTI-EXPERTTHINKER •

Now let's consider what happens when a company successfully fights Groupthink and ExpertThink tendencies. Consider Apple Computer.

In May of 1998 Apple Computer introduced the very stylish, the very colorful iMac (Figure 3-3). The decision to introduce the iMac was bold. It went against the most sacred tenet of Expert-Think in the PC industry: Functionality is king.

Figure 3-3. The original iMac.

I'll take a good-natured poke at my own industry by questioning what the reaction would have been if "Joe Smith" from the marketing department had walked into a group of engineers at IBM or Dell or even Intel in 1995 (three years before iMac), and suggested that a "cool form factor" could be a competitive differentiator in the PC, on par with functionality. I think most of those engineers would have laughed poor Joe Smith right out of their little gray cubicles.

But Apple ignored industry ExpertThink, and with great success. According to the market research firm PC Data, Apple's U.S. retail market share increased from 6.8 percent in July of 1998 to 13.5 percent in August of that year.[16] And *BusinessWeek* stated that "The eye-catching iMac is reviving a feeling that Apple Computer has not been able to spark in years: love between consumer and computer."[17] Even Bill Gates, of Apple's arch-rival Microsoft, gushed over the iMac saying, "To create a new standard it takes something that's not just a little bit different. It takes something that's really new and really captures people's imagination. And the Macintosh, of all the machines I've ever seen, is the only one that meets that standard."

This innovative thinking has continued at the company and encompasses form and function in such products as the iPod (Apple's runaway market-leading MP3 player), which was credited in 2004 with more than tripling Apple's stock. Interestingly, the perception of Apple as a nonconformist company has served it well. The company's willingness to thumb its nose at convention is often credited with being one of its primary brand strengths.

What's the cost of Groupthink and ExpertThink? Missing out on a new product category like disposable diapers. Missing out on the type of success Apple is currently experiencing.

Time to do something about it.

The ties that bind are the ties that blind.[18] — *Andrew Hargadon*

• KEY POINTS •

1. ExpertThink is the tendency people have to make decisions based on their own expertise, the opinions of other experts, or the mindset of those in authority.

2. Successful organizations and industries are particularly suscepti-ble to ExpertThink and the damaging effect it can have on innova-tion.

3. A prerequisite for successful innovation may be to break away from ExpertThink.

PART II

....

ZERO-GRAVITY THINKERS

Question: If what we know kills innovation, then how can we safeguard against it for our most crucial challenges?

Answer: Temporarily introduce one (or more) Zero-Gravity Thinkers to our teams.

Zero-Gravity Thinkers are team members (individuals or sometimes an outside group of people) who help us escape the weight of what we know. In Part III of this book we will discuss the roles they can play and when they should play them, but this portion of the book is devoted to describing who Zero-Gravity Thinkers are. Helping teams defy gravity after all, isn't something just anyone can do.

The Zero-Gravity Thinker has three primary characteristics: psychological distance from the team, renaissance tendencies, and related expertise as it pertains to the challenge (Figure II-1). The optimal Zero-Gravity Thinker has a blend of these three characteristics.

Figure II-1. Zero-Gravity Thinker.

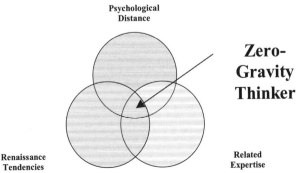

Chapter 4 provides an overview of psychological distance and its benefit in fighting Groupthink. Chapter 5 defines renaissance tendencies (the predisposition toward being passionate about learning new things and highly inventive) and discusses the value of this characteristic in stimulating innovative thinking. And Chapter 6 outlines related expertise: experience or knowledge that makes a person "smart-enough-to-understand-the-basics" of a challenge but not so thoroughly immersed in a field or discipline to be a victim of ExpertThink.

CHAPTER 4

TIME TRAVEL TO SEE THE NAKED EMPEROR

THE BENEFIT OF PSYCHOLOGICAL DISTANCE

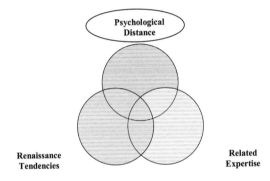

NEARLY EVERYONE IS FAMILIAR with the story "The Emperor's New Clothes," but I invite you to revisit your childhood and take a moment to refamiliarize yourself with it since it makes a point relevant to psychological distance.

The parallel between this story and the topic of this book is obvious. No one wanted to look stupid (or incompetent) and so everyone ignored their own best judgment and went along with the crowd. (Hans Christian Andersen adapted this story in the mid-1800s from an even older Spanish tale. Human nature hasn't changed much, has it?) The point I want to make though is that the hero of this story, the person who gives everyone permission to speak their mind, is a child.

So what does that have to do with stimulating innovative

thinking in companies? Should we revoke some of those child labor laws? Should Zero-Gravity Thinkers be children? Well, no. But, if you accept the notion that we are all hampered in our ability to regularly challenge the status quo (whether in groups or even in our own minds), then it makes sense to consider that a childlike challenge to our thinking may, in fact, be just what we need. The child in this fairy tale plays the catalytic role because he is outside the adult social hierarchy and isn't worried about losing social standing by speaking up. He doesn't know or care about the "norms" of good social behavior. He brings the value of psychological distance to the situation. And psychological distance is the nemesis of Groupthink.

▶The Emperor's New Clothes

(Adapted from the Hans Christian Andersen story)

Many years ago there lived an Emperor who loved nothing more than fine new clothes. One day two swindlers posing as tailors approached him. They said they could make him the most beautiful set of clothes in the world out of a marvelous new cloth. The cloth, they said, was not only beautiful but also unique in that it could not be seen by those who were stupid or unfit for their positions.

The Emperor paid the tailors a large sum of money to make him a set of clothes from this magical fabric.

Over the next several days the tailors pretended to work at their looms. They called for the finest silks and went through the motions of toiling deep into the evening as if weaving diligently.

After several days, the Emperor was eager to hear of their progress, so he sent his most trusted minister to visit the tailors. Of course, when the minister entered the room in which the tailors were working, he could see nothing. The skilled swindlers pantomimed holding up yards of fabric for the minister's inspection and the minister remarked favorably on their progress. But secretly he was mortified.

"The Emperor must never know that I cannot see a thing or I will be dismissed from my post," he thought. And so the old minister reported back to the Emperor that the fabric was indeed the most elegant and gorgeous he had ever seen, and the Emperor was satisfied.

Several more days passed and the tailors requested more silk and continued to work their empty looms. Once again the Emperor became eager for a progress report and decided to send another of his trusted advisors. Of course this faithful servant had an experience very similar to the minister before him. And, though he had seen nothing but an elaborate act by the swindler tailors, he reported solid progress on the "finest suit of clothes the world has ever seen."

Finally the day arrived for the clothes to be finished and the Emperor himself went to try them on. With great fanfare and elaborate care, the swindlers helped the Emperor into his make-believe shirt and pants and cape.

"Oh, your majesty," they gushed, "you are magnificent in this finery. Your subjects will be in awe."

"Yes, indeed," the Emperor's courtiers echoed as they stared at their sovereign in his underwear, "these clothes are the most magnificent you have ever worn."

The Emperor stared at his reflection in the mirror and tried not to show his discomfort. Surely he was not an idiot or unfit for office. Surely if he looked long enough he would be able to see the clothes the tailors had so carefully dressed him in.

Finally the Emperor did the only thing he felt he could do. He smiled at his reflection, thanked the tailors profusely for their efforts, and announced to his court that he was ready to walk with a procession through the streets so that all of his subjects might admire his finery.

The tailors made a big fuss about carrying the train of his cape. The courtiers marched regally by his side and the Emperor strode proudly through the streets of his kingdom in nothing but his undergarments.

People lined the streets to see the procession, since all had heard of the clothes that only those who were clever could see. Murmurs of appreciation were heard all along the procession route.

"Look at how the cloth shimmers in the sun," said one.

"The cut and fit are extraordinary," said another.

No one wanted to state the truth until the procession passed a small child.

"But Papa," the child said loudly, "he has nothing on."

Suddenly it was as if the child's voice had opened a floodgate and the entire crowd started to whisper that the Emperor had on no clothes. When the whispering finally reached the ears of the Emperor and his courtiers,

the Emperor quickly turned and raced back to his palace

for he knew the truth and was greatly embarrassed to

have been such a fool in front of his subjects. ■

PSYCHOLOGICAL DISTANCE: GROUPTHINK'S NEMESIS

As I was researching psychological distance, one of the interesting articles I found was from a *New York Times* piece highlighting the story of a soldier in 1968 named Hugh Thompson, who was flying over a Vietnam village in a helicopter as American troops on the ground were attacking its residents. [1] The soldiers had been told that the town was a Vietcong stronghold. But Thompson could see there was no enemy return fire. The village was completely civilian. He ended up landing his helicopter, rescuing some of the villagers and telling his commanders about the massacre. Thompson was a whistle-blower. As it turns out, whistle-blowers have a lot in common with the child in the Emperor story.

Whistle-blowers are often people who are psychologically distanced from a situation. As Princeton professor John Darley states in the *Times* article, "Someone who didn't get caught up in the start, someone who walks in and hasn't been involved in the escalation, like pilot Thompson, can see the process for what it really is." Like a child who isn't part of the social hierarchy, a whistle-blower doesn't feel like part of the group they expose. This is why psychological distance can often disrupt Groupthink. There is a greater likelihood of participating in Groupthink if you are part of the group. Outsiders, though not entirely immune, have a higher level of resistance.

I'm not suggesting that whistle-blowers are the way to sustain innovation. I do believe, however, that detachment can result in new ways of viewing a situation that are highly valuable. If you've read a management or innovation book in the last ten years, you've read about the importance of hiring such detached employees to spark innovative thinking. Stanford Business School professor Robert Sutton, for example, advocates hiring loners, agitators, and people who are slow to learn (or accept) the norms of organizational culture.[2] This advice is echoed by University of California at Berkeley psychology professor Charlan Jeanne Nemeth, who advocates hiring creative people who will provide minority opinions that disrupt the corporate mindset.[3]

Making these people permanent members of the team can help create an innovation-friendly culture. But, adding temporary outsiders to the mix can provide additional benefit for two reasons:

1. Most people (even the most radical thinkers) have great difficulty being insiders and outsiders at the same time.
2. Even those people who can play the insider/outsider balancing act can't typically sustain it forever.

THE PERILS OF BEING AN
• INSIDER AND AN OUTSIDER •
AT THE SAME TIME

I once participated in discussions with a group regarding future projections for product revenue. The general manager (GM) was under intense pressure from his investors to meet forecasts he had made when the group was founded. If he couldn't show a plan that at least came close to his earlier predictions, not only would his credibility be damaged, but in all likelihood the entire group would lose significant funding and investor support.

Over the course of a week his senior managers evaluated every option available to them to no avail. Each of them believed that the new projections had to be nearly half of the previous ones. But this answer was unacceptable to the GM.

In a final meeting in which his senior staff each voiced their strong support for a lower forecast, the GM lost his temper and invited anyone who couldn't believe in the business opportunity as he did to tender their resignation. He accused the team of being traitors to the vision or simply lazy cowards—unwilling to set a tough goal and then work hard to achieve it.

At that particular moment, there was little choice. The GM's managers could either have agreed to the higher forecast or started looking for other jobs. Well, with mortgages, new babies, orthodontia, college tuition, and even retirement to think of, every manager in the room ended up voicing their support for the more aggressive forecast. Many of them later started quietly circulating their resumes. But by then the damage had been done. The GM submitted the aggressive forecast truly believing that his management team had "seen the light" and was behind the plan. Blinded by worries for his own job, he looked on his loss of temper as a positive occurrence that had reinvigorated his team. He didn't seem to realize he had simply bullied his subordinates into going along with him. This was unfortunate for everyone because, as it later turned out, the business couldn't meet its forecast, and investor support was so severely damaged that most of the management team ended up being replaced.

This is a radical example of why insiders have a hard time playing the role of outsiders. They have too little psychological distance. Their livelihoods are based on being part of the team over the long-term, forcing them to sometimes make compromises that are suboptimal. In this situation the managers pushed and argued their points as far as they dared. But in the end, when faced with the prospect of being ostracized from the team (by being fired), they caved in—as many of us would in similar circumstances.

I can think of numerous times when I've stopped arguing with a boss or peer because I was "choosing my battles." Heck, I do this with my daughter all of the time. As the twentieth-century American poet Phyllis McGinley said:

Compromise, if not the spice of life, is its solidity. It is what makes nations great and marriages happy.[4]

But compromise, while a necessity in marriage, politics, and even business, can be devastating to innovation, particularly when it is coerced by the group or the boss or even industry peers. Often it seems that innovators have to hold their ground and bear the scorn of those around them until the value of their ideas can be proven. Take a look at the case of Dr. John Floyd, who persevered with his innovation work in tin smelting despite the lack of support from colleagues and industry cohorts.

The Innovator the Experts Panned

In the 1970s, Melbourne metallurgist Dr. John Floyd had a radical idea for improving smelting—the process of extracting a metal from its ore by heating and chemical reduction.

His idea was to inject reducing gases into the liquid metal ore (called slag) using a metal steel lance. Industry experts and colleagues were fiercely skeptical: "In 1970 no one believed that what I was doing would work. By 1975 I had perhaps 1 percent support. By 1980 it was 10 percent," said Floyd.

The process is now called Sirosmelt.

Today, over thirty percent of the world's tin is produced by Sirosmelt. And the Dandenong-based company Ausmelt, created to commercialize the technology, has commissioned plants operating across Asia, Europe, Southern Africa, and South America.[5]

Bucking Conventional Wisdom in Real Estate

Or consider the case of real estate guru, R. Scot Sellers who blithely ignores the collective wisdom of other real estate experts to the benefit of the entire industry.

R. Scot Sellers is the chairman and CEO of Armstrong-Smith, one of the nation's largest apartment investment and operations companies. With a market capitalization of $11.8 billion in early

2005 and the distinction of being recognized by *Fortune* Magazine in 2004 as one of America's Most Admired Companies, Armstrong-Smith seems to have found the secret to success—continuously breaking all of the rules.

Just two of Sellers' numerous innovations include:

1. Spearheading the use of the Web for tenant credit screening. "People said it wouldn't work, but we proved it did, and now [most owners and managers] can't imagine life without it," Sellers said.

2. Pioneering the approach (previously unheard of in the real estate industry) of acquiring or developing properties in high-barrier-to-entry markets. "We were laughed at in 1995 for this strategy," said Sellers. "To see now the industry-wide acceptance of it as the wise thing to do is pretty interesting."[6]

The experiences of Floyd and Sellers offer just two examples of how sticking with an unpopular or even ridiculed idea might be a prerequisite for innovation. Unfortunately, most insiders have too much at stake to consistently battle the boss, the rest of the team, or even their industry peers. Remember what Arthur Schlesinger said regarding why he didn't speak up more forcefully during the Bay of Pigs discussion? "A course of objection would have accomplished little save gain me a name as a nuisance."[7]

This isn't to say that coercion is the only reason the inside-outsider balancing act is so challenging. The fact is that over time most people start to have a lot more in common with people they work with than people they don't. Think of the typical senior executive management team. Most members probably have similar income levels, similar levels of education, and similar career experiences—typically having worked for the same company for many years. Regardless of how different these people may look on the outside (and often even those differences are relatively minor), they have all been "assimilated," as the characters in the TV show *Star Trek* would say.

In fact, studies conducted by Donald Pelz and Frank Andrews

found that heterogeneous, interdisciplinary groups became homogenous in the way they approach problems after three years together.[8] (In many groups I'd say this happens long before the three-year mark!) By then norms and best known methods have kicked in to help things move smoothly and efficiently. Unfortunately, by losing the rough edges and messy inefficiencies that groups start off with, they also tend to lose the out-of-left-field-ideas and radical thinking that they were trying to get by bringing different people together in the first place!

• THE CHALLENGE OF THE PERMANENT • BALANCING ACT

Of course there are some permanent insiders who do successfully play a devil's advocate role. Leaders however, need to remember two things when it comes to relying on these people to act as innovation catalysts over the long term. First, these individuals are at high risk of feeling alone and getting burned out. Professor Nemeth's research states that the "highly creative" individual includes personality traits such as confidence and independence, a preference for complexity over simplicity, preferring some disorder over everything neat and tidy, and a tendency for being "childlike though not childish."[9] She further states that these personality traits don't typically fit well within most corporate cultures. As a result, there is a very real risk that these people will feel (and be) isolated.

A great example of this is a friend of mine who is a highly artistic, free thinker and who also happens to be an expert in the field of organizational development. Maggie was hired by Intel because she had such a unique approach to help establish a new group within the company. Everyone loved her. She was like a breath of fresh air walking down the gray cubicle-lined halls, with her curly red hair, her bohemian-style clothing, and her wide friendly smile. Better still, Maggie's ideas were just as fresh as she was. Sure, she had a lot of crazy ones, many of which were never implemented. But she also had some great ones, and she was learning to work within the system to get those great ideas realized.

In general people felt good about having Maggie around. But Maggie wasn't so happy. Yes, she was learning to work within the bureaucracy of a large corporation, and yes she was having successes. But she perceived the cost to her as far too great. "I feel like this place is going to suck the life right out of me," she said. Maggie felt that she was so different from the norm that it was exhausting to either "buck the system" constantly or pretend to be something other than what she was. In the end, Maggie left after about two years with the company.

Maggie's experience illustrates the very real challenge "different thinkers" face as they strive to be successful in organizations. Whether they choose to "conform-to-the-norm" or remain true to themselves, they must exert a tremendous amount of energy. And, in the end, many find it too taxing.

The second thing leaders need to keep in mind is that different thinkers are typically not so different from anyone else. They too have mortgages and college tuition to think about. They too learn that working with a group sometimes requires compromise. And, for companies to assume that these folks can always be depended on for the contrary point of view is unfair and unrealistic. Over time the free-thinkers that companies do manage to retain tend to get assimilated—just like everyone else.

The book *Classics in the History of Psychology* states that "At the psychological level . . . the individual becomes a group member to the extent that he internalizes the major norms of the group, carries on the responsibilities, and meets expectations for the position he occupies."[10] With that definition in mind, it could be that most outsiders (even the wildest and wackiest thinkers) really start becoming insiders the day they are hired. They simply lose psychological distance.

Psychological distance is an important Zero-Gravity-Thinker characteristic because it is one of the most effective weapons against Groupthink. Too often we assume we have instilled diverse thinking into our organizations by building teams of varied functional backgrounds, genders, ethnicity, etc. What we tend to forget is that if these people all come from our same organization, they are likely to have a more similar mindset than we might believe. Adding a temporary psychological outsider to the mix once in a while keeps us honest about whether or not the Emperor is wearing clothes.

Wild Ducks

There was a man who liked to watch the ducks in his pond each fall. Well intentioned, he began to feed them, only to find that, with time, they stopped flying south. They wintered in the pond, feeding on what he provided. After several years, they grew so fat and lazy that they hardly flew at all (Figure 4-1).

Figure 4-1.

The message is that we can hire "different" thinkers to permanently join us, but they aren't likely to stay different thinkers for long: They become "domesticated." In other words: You can make wild ducks tame, but you can never make tame ducks wild again."

• KEY POINTS •

1. A person with psychological distance doesn't feel like part of the group they may be working with. These people are better able than others to resist Groupthink.

2. People who are successful innovators often have psychological distance from the group, organization, or industry they are impacting.

3. Most people can't maintain psychological distance for long once they begin working for or within an organization, team, or industry. Therefore, organizations that want to disrupt Groupthink and stimulate innovative thinking can benefit from temporarily bringing in outsiders with this characteristic.

CHAPTER 5

JUST CURIOUS

THE BENEFIT OF RENAISSANCE TENDENCIES

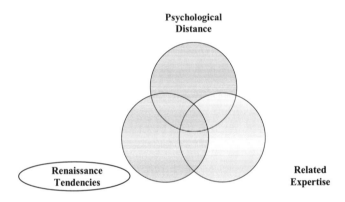

HERMAN D'HOOGE is a brilliant colleague of mine at Intel, who is dedicated to increasing the company's innovation efforts as they pertain to the needs of technology users—people, in other words. He has been instrumental in the development of multiple new concepts at Intel that have and will change the way people interact with technology. And because those efforts have been successful, people listen to him.

But these days just by listening to Herman for a short time, you'd never guess that his background is in engineering. Instead, he sounds more like an ethnographer or social anthropologist or even an industrial designer as he philosophizes about how people need and want to interact with the machines that house Intel's technology. Herman has evolved from thinking that if an engineer builds a better mousetrap the world will beat a path to his door to thinking that an engineer had better figure out first whether the world even wants a better mousetrap and then determine exactly what kind of mousetrap the world would be most likely to buy before even considering whether or how to build it.

For him the big epiphany that engineers don't know everything there is to know about developing new technologies came after he spent a great deal of the 1990s developing a telephony technology for PCs. Though the end-result was technically sound, no one wanted it. Using the PC for telephone calls, at least in the manner his team had envisioned, was more trouble than it was worth. Herman realized with great dismay that he had just wasted a lot of his career on something that was meaningless.

The impact of that realization was significant because it started him on the path toward becoming more attune to the needs of people than to the possibilities of technology. What he began looking for were intersections between the two. And over time his search for intersections led him to the belief that the more experiences and information you can soak in, the greater the likelihood that you will stumble across something meaningful.

"I will meet with anybody," he says of the way he spends his time. "The problem with most companies is that people aren't encouraged to do that. They are too myopic, only focused on what they need to deliver today or tomorrow. People aren't willing to 'waste time' so they don't explore outside their own limited boundaries." Innovation, Herman believes, requires regular exploration beyond one's boundaries. Herman has "renaissance tendencies."

The familiar term "Renaissance Man" is used to describe someone who has broad interests and capabilities; a generalist essentially. It dates back to the period between approximately A.D. 1300 to 1500, when science, art and intellectual exploration flourished. This is the period that gave us Leonardo da Vinci, who made contributions in art, science, and biology, and who is even credited with conceiving of the bicycle and airplane! His curiosity and intellect led him to explore well outside the confines of his original training as a painter. In fact it is the wide nature of his explorations that are likely to have given him many of the insights that fueled his work.

Someone with renaissance tendencies (which I use as more of a gender-agnostic term) may not be another Leonardo in the making but is inclined to have broad interests in a wide variety of fields. In fact, research suggests that the most innovative thinkers tend to be people who are open-minded, well traveled, well hobbied, and well read. They are people who show a natural curiosity, a yearn-to-learn, and a penchant for seeking out different experiences (professionally and personally). They are more likely to draw creative connections between objects and ideas, in part because they have been exposed to so many. Nobel-Prize-winning physicist Arthur Scawlow summed it up well when he said, "The most successful scientists often are not the most talented, but the ones who are just impelled by curiosity."[1]

> The most successful scientists often are not the most talented, but the ones who are just impelled by curiosity.
— Arthur Scawlow ■

Lewis Terman, a Stanford University psychologist, has conducted studies supporting the notion that broad exposure to ideas and experiences fosters creativity. He conducted research on over 1,000 intellectually gifted children and focused particular attention on their home environments. Not surprising is the fact that his work found that intellectually gifted people tend to grow up in homes where parents value and support learning through exposure to a wide range of stimulation. Their homes are typically ripe with books and magazines, and their leisure time is frequently filled with trips to museums, cultural exhibits, libraries, etc. What is particularly interesting in this research, however, is the finding that the children who grow up to become notable for their creative achievements tend to come from homes that are the most stimulation-rich. In addition to exposure to museums and concerts and a plethora of reading material, these creative overachievers (artists, musicians, writers, etc.) are also likely to have traveled extensively (domestically and internationally) and to have been raised by parents who exposed them to "different" ideas as a result of their having less-conventional occupations and interests.

Exposure to new situations and even familiar information presented in new ways helps break down our mindsets. A group of gifted artists selected from a national competition by the Yale School of Art participated in an experiment conducted by psychiatrist Albert Rothenberg. These artists were shown highly incongruent images superimposed on each other. For instance a four-poster bed was shown in a French period room juxtaposed over a group of soldiers taking cover from enemy fire behind a tank. The artists were then asked to create pastel drawings inspired by these images. The result was compelling. An independent panel rated the drawings of those who had been exposed to these juxtaposed images as far more creative than work completed by artists who had been exposed to the same images shown to them separately.[2] The unusual combinations apparently disrupted the traditional mindset these images would typically have triggered. And this phenomenon extends beyond the world of art into the world of business.

• A REAL-LIFE STUDY IN CONTRAST •

Meet Chris Riley, a real-life example of someone who creates value at the intersection of incongruent ideas. Chris is the founder of brand and strategy consultancy Studioriley. It is July 2005, and Chris, who was formerly the chief strategic officer for advertising powerhouse Wieden + Kennedy, is sitting in a coffee house with me in Portland, Oregon. During his career Chris has been an influential player (along with great creative teams, he reminds me) in building some of the most powerful brands in the world, including Nike, Coca-Cola, Microsoft, and Apple. Yet, as he sits next to me in an overstuffed chair wearing shorts and sipping his coffee, he reminds me more of a professor or artist than a high-powered executive. In part, I know this is because of where we are sitting.

Chris has chosen the place for our meeting, World Cup Coffee, a company dedicated to the environmentally and socially responsible sourcing and sale of its product. This particular café in the company's chain is located in the EcoTrust Building in downtown Portland, a renovated warehouse that is now home to retailers, companies, and organizations that make environmental sustainability a focal point of their business mission. Surrounded by all of this environmentalism, I almost feel guilty talking about ways to help companies make more money through innovation. Philosophizing about academia, art, politics, or the plight of the Third World would have seemed more appropriate.

Nevertheless, we spend a pleasant hour swapping stories of how innovative thinking is inspired and I share with him the three characteristics I believe a Zero-Gravity Thinker should have. Chris nods his head in agreement as I explain each one, but then tells me with great conviction that "renaissance tendencies are by far the most important." When I press him on this, he tells me that exposing oneself to a vast array of new things—ideas, concepts, and experiences—is a prerequisite for actually doing new things.

It doesn't dawn on me until later, when I spend some quality time exploring the Studioriley website (studioriley.com), that what I found slightly jarring about the juxtaposition of our "capitalist" conversation with World Cup Coffee's eco-atmosphere was exactly the sort of collision between worlds that Chris lives every day.

Chris is passionately devoted to the belief that social accountability has become a requirement for a healthy brand. During our meeting he related the story of a focus group he attended while working with Nike in which a young man not only knew the country in which a pair of shoes had been manufactured, he actually knew the factory. Chris believes that consumers will increasingly care about such things. Social and environmental responsibility may have traditionally been at odds with big business but today he believes they are synergistic.

Chris communicates this synergy on his website while also giving visitors a peek at his renaissance tendencies. What I first noticed as I scanned the site after our conversation was that it looks nothing like most others. Instead of being laid out in a boxy format with the most visible icons being easy navigation buttons to this or that idea or concept, it reads more like the diary of an explorer, inventor, and philosopher. Interspersed among photos and trip notes from around the world are musings on the beauty of industrial design and assorted quotes from such diverse people as Pope John Paul II, Johnny Cash, and Bob Marley. The effect of this eclectic collage is to, well . . . make you think. By juxtaposing evocative images and ideas, Chris coaxes site visitors to entertain a mindset shift. Perhaps there is a profound synergy between a responsibility for the world we live in and the way we earn our living.

At any rate, the fact that Chris borrows from so many incongruent worlds to convey his thoughts is testament to his constant search for new stimuli. Chris's renaissance tendencies have put him in the middle of new kind of intersection. And, with clients like Apple and Nokia among the converted, it looks to be a flourishing one as well.

(Note: Just before the completion of this book, Chris accepted an invitation to bring his Zero-Gravity-Thinker characteristics to Apple on a permanent basis. Of all the organizations that might be able to capitalize on his unique perspective over the long term, Apple is undoubtedly one of the best.)

• UNEXPECTED ASSOCIATIONS •

But can just anyone enhance their creative capabilities by exposing themselves to "what's new"? Probably. But, I'd add a caveat. I believe that some people simply have a greater innate ability to be creative and innovative than others. And these are the types of people you want to find to play Zero-Gravity-Thinker roles for your team.

A 2003 study published by University of Toronto and Harvard University psychologists[3] highlights the innate differences between highly creative people and those who are less so. The study looked at something called latent inhibition. *Latent inhibition* is the unconscious capacity most of us have to ignore stimuli that are irrelevant to whatever task or situation we are facing. Most mothers, for instance, become adept at tuning out the happy but loud shrieks of their playing children in order to have a conversation with the mother sitting next to them on a park bench. Most of us who work in cubicles learn to ignore, at least to a large degree, the conversations of coworkers in the cubicles next to us. If our brains don't recognize it as relevant to what we are doing, latent inhibition allows us to filter it out, an ability that can be highly valuable in helping us think logically and deliver tangible end-results.

The Toronto/Harvard study found, however, that some of us have filters that are less discriminating than others. It found that people who are deemed to be highly creative tend to be more open than others to thinking about environmental stimuli in unexpected ways. These people have low latent inhibition. For instance, those of us who are less creative (with high latent inhibition) tend to classify (or mentally file) concepts or objects as soon as we see them. As an example, the mother in the park hears the sounds her children are making and her brain automatically classifies them as harmless. Unless something changes, she is unlikely to spend any more brainpower even considering those sounds.

Here's another example. Most Westerners know that a fork is a utensil for eating. When those of us with high latent inhibition see one at a restaurant, we classify it and don't bother to consider it again except as a tool for getting food from our plates to our mouths. We certainly don't think about it when we want to take a drink or use the restroom. In fact, we are likely to think about it again only when the problem we are facing is associated with something that reminds us of eating.

Highly creative people on the other hand tend not to classify or associate as rigidly as other people. Those of us in this camp have the equivalent of a very lax filing system. Subsequently, because we are less likely to strongly associate one stimulus with another, we aren't as likely to predetermine what is and isn't relevant to a particular challenge. This means that when we are trying to solve a problem we may mentally revisit a huge range of stimuli over and again. Accounting challenge? Tadpole. Calculator. Table. Socrates. Fork. By exposing highly creative people (who also have high intelligence and a strong memory) to a large amount of stimuli, the resulting ideas are likely to be far more creative than if you expose less-creative people to the same things.[4]

It's worth noting that, as discussed earlier, at its extreme an inability to associate objects and ideas with a mindset is akin to some forms of autism and can be highly debilitating. In fact, the Toronto/Harvard study suggests (as have others) the link between mental illness and creativity. The study notes that chemical changes during the early stages of schizophrenia often lead to an inability to screen out stimuli leading to feelings of deep insight and mystical knowledge. Latent inhibition is not just low during this period, it essentially disappears.

I don't suggest that the Zero-Gravity Thinkers you bring into your organization have mental challenges such as these. But, perhaps there are degrees of latent inhibition (Figure 5-1). Autistic individuals and some schizophrenics may be at one end of the spectrum. People with lower levels of creativity might be on the other side. And the highly creative who can help you in the Zero-Gravity-Thinker role might reside somewhere in between.

• MEASURING RENAISSANCE TENDENCIES •

How do you measure renaissance tendencies? Latent inhibition studies are enlightening, but as of this writing they don't offer a

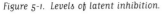
Figure 5-1. Levels of latent inhibition.

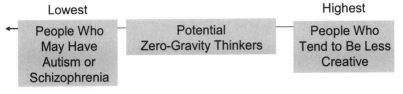

practical quantitative method (outside of a university setting) for leaders to use in screening Zero-Gravity Thinkers. In the future that may change, and other methodologies may become practical tools as well.

For instance, at the Centre for the Mind, the joint venture of the Australian National University and the University of Sydney that was mentioned in Chapter 3, Professor Allan Snyder and his team are researching a methodology for determining a person's ideation fluency through a measure called the Creativity Quotient (CQ). In many ways, measuring a person's CQ is a lot like measuring whether they have high or low levels of latent inhibition. In other words, are they highly creative or not?

According to Snyder, the test is based on the premise that fluency, flexibility, and originality of ideas are all indicators of creative capacity. CQ is evaluated based on a timed test in which participants are asked to list as many uses for a particular item as they can. Responses are then evaluated based not only on their total number, but on the number of categories they fall into as well.

In one example, participants were asked to suggest all possible uses for a piece of paper within five minutes. Writing, painting and drawing were all grouped into the same category (using paper as a surface to mark on). The suggestion to use paper as a hat was classified in a completely different category (using paper as clothing).

In Snyder's methodology suggestions in new categories are weighted more heavily than additional suggestions in existing categories. The idea being that coming up with new categories requires more innovative thought. It is likely that the people who have the highest CQ scores on Snyder's test would also have low latent inhibition (allowing them to combine ideas in unexpected ways) and strong renaissance tendencies (meaning they have exposed themselves to a lot of ideas). Snyder and his team are still completing research on the test and its potential for real-world application.

In the meantime, making a qualitative judgment about someone's renaissance tendencies may not be as difficult as it seems. Sometimes even a short conversation is enough. An hour-long discussion, for instance, with Chris Riley or my Intel colleague Herman D'Hooge, both of whom are quite outgoing, is sufficient to uncover their strong renaissance tendencies.

Assessing the renaissance tendencies of quieter individuals on the other hand can require a little more work. My dad is a good example. For as long as I can remember, he has explored new ideas and come up with all sorts of interesting (and sometimes wacky) inventions. One year when we lived on a strawberry farm, he tore apart an old wheat combine and rigged it up to become a makeshift strawberry picker. Another year he tinkered with fans and deodorizing agents to develop an electric gadget that he installed behind the toilets in my parents' house. He called it the CommOdorEater. It's still there and their bathroom always smells fresh! And in between inventions he reads about the stock market, the latest health discoveries, and . . . well, the list goes on and on. My dad definitely has renaissance tendencies, but unless you asked him the right questions or happened to see one of his inventions, you'd never know it.

The Right Questions

We look for smart. Smart as in "Do they do something weird outside of work, something off the beaten path?" That translates into people who have no fear of trying difficult projects and going outside the bounds of what they know.[5] — *Wayne Rosing, head of engineering at Google*

What are the right questions? They fall into two general categories: The first is *innovative capability*. Has the person demonstrated a notable level of innovative thinking that required the combination of new ideas or concepts? Did they translate their innovative thinking into some type of action or tangible result and/or did they share their thoughts or insights with others in some form or fashion? A person doesn't have to have creative successes under their belt in order to demonstrate innovative capability. But they should be able to demonstrate the ability to conceive of a creative idea and then translate it into something that can at least be shared with others.

The second is *passion-for-learning*. Has the person demonstrated a notable level of curiosity and passion for learning about many new ideas and concepts? Ask them to elaborate on two or three things they've learned or done in the past year that they considered fascinating or eye-opening. Why did they become enthralled with the topic? Were they curious enough to scratch beneath the surface? Did they read, visit, experiment, etc., to satisfy their curiosity? Expand the discussion to the past five years. What other things have they considered interesting? Did they explore those things in any depth? What hobbies or activities has this person been involved with in that time? What kinds of jobs has this person had? Listen for passion. Listen for variety.

If one purpose of a Zero-Gravity Thinker is to inspire innovative thinking in a team, then perhaps Chris Riley is right when he says that renaissance tendencies are the most important characteristic this temporary team member needs to contribute. After all, how can one who is not innovative inspire it in others?

Renaissance tendencies fuel imagination.

> I am enough of an artist to draw freely upon my imagination. Imagination is more important than knowledge. Knowledge is limited. Imagination encircles the world.
> — Albert Einstein ∎

• KEY POINTS •

1. A person with renaissance tendencies has a passion for learning, tends to have broad interests and/or hobbies, and has strong innovative-thinking capabilities.

2. People of high intelligence with renaissance tendencies are often able to connect seemingly disparate ideas in new, insightful, and valuable ways.

3. Renaissance tendencies may be the most important Zero-Gravity-Thinker characteristic because they allow people to see the world in a different way and inspire others to see the world differently as well.

CHAPTER 6

SMART ABOUT SOMETHING ELSE

THE BENEFIT OF RELATED EXPERTISE

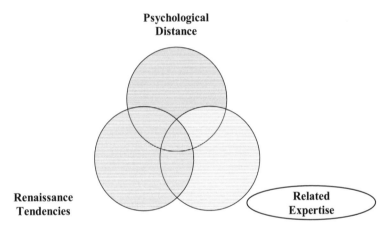

WE ALMOST HAVE a complete picture of the Zero-Gravity Thinker. To recap, psychological distance foils Groupthink, and renaissance tendencies fuel imagination. So, what does the last characteristic, related expertise, do? It disrupts ExpertThink.

Related expertise is just what it suggests: expertise in an area that is relevant but not specific to the challenge at hand. The objective of related expertise is not to weigh down the team with more of what they are already likely to know. It is to inspire them to explore the world from the perspective of what they don't know. Related expertise does this by introducing two factors: Naiveté and A Potential-Intersection Point.

• NAIVETÉ •

The word "naive" is derived from the Latin word *nativus*, which means "to be born." People who are naive view the world with the fresh eyes of someone who is new to the world, someone who has not yet been jaded. The word naive is synonymous with the words "beginner" and "novice." Teams that invite this perspective into their midst are sometimes surprised, however, to find it can also mean "insightful."

One example of the ability of those who are naive to stimulate valuable insights is recounted by Jeff Mauzy and Richard Harriman of the innovation consulting firm, Synectics. In their book, *Creativity, Inc.*, they talk of their experience with an oil company that was looking for a way to reduce the costs of bringing mixed fluid reservoirs (deposits of oil mixed with water) to the surface. The engineers on the team had tried for some time to come up with a good solution to this expensive problem, without success. Therefore, when the suggestion was made to revisit an idea that had always seemed promising but had never been realized, the engineers felt they had nothing to lose. They decided to re-explore the old concept of separating oil from water below ground so that only the cost of pumping oil to the surface would be incurred. The approach they decided to use for addressing this problem however was new. Instead of wrestling with the challenge solely amongst themselves, they invited outsiders in—outsiders from both inside and outside the petroleum industry. By the end of working with this combined team of experts and relatively naive outsiders, the petroleum company's engineers had over a dozen promising, previously unconsidered ideas for further exploration.[1]

Related experts bring a level of naiveté regarding some key aspect of the challenge into a team. And evidence that this can be beneficial is not just anecdotal. Scott Page, a political scientist at the University of Michigan, has introduced a mathematical argument stating that a mix of people—*experts* + *nonexperts-who-are-smart-enough-to-understand-the-basics*—will fare better at solving a complex problem than a group composed only of experts. Page stumbled across what he calls "this very unintuitive finding" in the mid-1990s, when he was an assistant professor of economics at the California Institute of Technology. He had been constructing computer models using "agents" to help solve complex problems. Depending on what was being studied, the agents could represent fish, firms, viruses, and even people. Through complex programming, the agents would interact with each other and their environments, according to sets of rules, in order to help predict such varied behavior as how flocks of birds migrate, how riots erupt, or how prices fluctuate in a market.

In one series of tests Page assigned some groups of agents with the programming equivalent of expertise-for-making-money in their simulated environment. He then compared the average performance of this expert-only group with the average performance of a random group of agents, some expert, some not—a mixed group, in other words. Though Page expected that the group composed only of experts would collectively fare better at money-making in the model, this was not the case. Surprisingly, the mixed group performed better. This initial finding led to years of careful, methodical research and Page's eventual belief that when problems are complex even the insertion of a single, smart nonexpert into a working group can have a positive impact on its performance.[2]

"The mathematics are overwhelmingly compelling," he said during a conversation I had with him. His conviction may be based on complicated mathematical formulae but it boils down to the fact that nonexperts bring different experiences and mindsets—tools, as he calls them—to the challenge from those brought by experts. And the more tools available to solve a problem, the better the ultimate solution is likely to be.

Nonexpert Tools + Expert Tools = More Tools = Better Solutions

• FUNNY MATH: TWO + TWO = FIVE •

By adding nonexperts to the mix we apply more tools to a problem. But that isn't their only impact. When there is significant interaction between experts and nonexperts on a team, something else happens as well. New tools are discovered or created.[3]

One reason for this is that novices make experts think differently. The power of teaching in problem solving is well documented. According to innovation researchers Mark and Barbara Stefik, "the process of explaining a problem or an idea to someone can fundamentally aid in thinking outside the box. . . . In general, the less familiar a second person is with our original problem, the more explanations we need to give. In this way, explaining a problem to someone else can help us to cultivate the beginner's mind and enable us to see the problem differently.[4]

I encountered a very basic example of this just a few nights ago. Frustrated that I couldn't figure out how to build a rather complex graph in an Excel spreadsheet, I mentioned the problem to my daughter, who is a freshman in high school. Smart as my daughter is, I knew she hadn't been graphing with Excel in her math class so I didn't expect her to be able to help me. Nevertheless, when she asked for more details of the problem, I decided to see what would happen if I explained it to her. Keep in mind that I had worked on this issue on and off for several hours that day and had asked several "Excel whizzes" I work with for help—all to no avail. But within three minutes (no exaggeration) of explaining the problem to my daughter, she asked me a simple question that changed my entire perspective. Based on that, you guessed it, I quickly figured out how to make my complicated graph. I also gave myself a little pat on the back for actually practicing what I preach.

Returning to Page's work (which, by the way, I have greatly simplified in this chapter), some might say that his belief that "mixed" groups are superior to homogenous groups for problem solving merely provides validation for the well established innovation management practice of forming diverse workgroups. Though it does do that, I believe it takes the concept one step further. Page's efforts suggest that the optimal diverse workgroup is not merely composed of people from different functional, industry, racial, or gender backgrounds. It is also composed of people with varying degrees of expertise and ability as related to the challenge at hand. It suggests that we should actively seek out and listen to those who are smart enough to speak our basic language but who are not (and may never be) fluent.[5]

> The optimal workgroup is composed of people with varying degrees of expertise and ability as related to the challenge at hand. ■

• A POTENTIAL INTERSECTION POINT •

What does it mean to be able to speak the basic language, to be (as the research suggests) "smart enough to understand the basics"? It means meeting the "calculus condition," meaning that if, for instance, the problem is related to calculus, the nonexpert has some understanding of calculus.[6] This basic familiarity allows a relative novice to stimulate innovative thinking not only based on her naiveté, but also based on her ability to apply different experience and knowledge to the situation. An outsider's ability to speak a "language" (even if it is only a rudimentary dialect) that others on the team understand facilitates the intersection of ideas from one realm to another.

This could have been called the finance condition, the biology condition, or, as the Ford case study below illustrates, the manufacturing condition.

In 1903 Henry Ford founded the Ford Motor Company and assembled a group of talented machinists and production engineers to manufacture the company's first cars. Over the next three years this group of early automotive experts steadily improved production techniques and established some of the world's first BKMs for automobile manufacturing in order to introduce car Models A, B, C, F, K, N, and R.

Three years later in 1906, however, those BMKs were stretched and re-formed by someone who had never built a car before. Walter E. Flanders was hired by Ford in August of that year. Borrowing from the manufacturing techniques he had encountered at a previous job with the Singer Manufacturing Company (makers of the famous sewing machine), Flanders introduced the concept of interchangeable production parts as an alternative to the custom parts that Ford and other auto industry experts were relying on.

The idea of interchangeable parts in the auto industry was radical. In 1906 automobiles were being built with parts developed in the tradition of European craftsman with plenty of hand work and what was referred to as "fitting" or customizing required to assemble the individual parts together. The automotive experts at Ford hadn't yet encountered the mass production techniques that the Singer Sewing Machine Company had spearheaded, in which highly uniform parts dramatically increased assembly speed and efficiency .(Information didn't travel at Internet speed in those days.) The idea that an axle or wheel made for one car would fit another of the same model without any custom adjustments was essentially unheard of.

But Henry Ford had open ears when it came to the wild ideas that Flanders with his sewing machine experience introduced. With Ford's support, Flanders was able to merge his previous experience with that of the existing Ford team, and together they found that interchangeable parts changed everything. With little custom fitting required during assembly, Ford's original process of putting a group of skilled craftsman together to hand-build one car at a time became obsolete. Premade, uniform parts meant that relatively unskilled workers could perform assembly work piecemeal without having to worry about how all of the parts would come together in the end.

Flanders and the team worked to capitalize on this efficiency. Instead of shuffling employees between parts and machinery, they devised ways to bring the now-uniform parts and machinery to the employees. The team placed machine tools and parts according to the sequential operations required to build a car, the precursor to the assembly line was born, and the Ford Motor Company's next car, the Model T, brought the automobile within financial reach of the average American.

In many ways the insertion of Flanders—as an outsider with related expertise—into the Ford team, established the foundation for today's auto society. But important as his contributions were while he was there, the residual impact of his presence may have been even more significant. Flanders stayed with Ford only temporarily, less than two years. However, it wasn't until several years later—on April 1, 1913—that Ford manufacturing experts introduced the first *moving* assembly line based on the work they had started with Flanders. The point is that Flanders was a key participant in the process as well as a catalyst for inspiring new insights on the team. Because of their relatively short-lived encounter with this "naive" outsider whose expertise intersected with their own, Ford's automotive design experts moved leaps and bounds beyond where they (and he) had been.[8]

A Related Expert Lights the Way

Here's a more recent example of the power of related expertise. Remember the red Eveready Flashlight that was almost a standard fixture in most American kitchens or garages in the last half of the twentieth century? Sales of that product had been fairly steady for the Eveready Battery Company for years when Ralston Purina acquired the organization in 1986. As far as Eveready's management was concerned, that red flashlight was akin to "Coca Cola"—an American icon that you just didn't mess with (OK, not messing with Coke is a whole 'nother story).

You can imagine the trepidation then when Peggy Cornwell, Ralston Purina's hand-picked product manager for the business (someone who had been selling pet foods and cereals in bright

▶ Radical Collaboration

"Radical collaboration" is how Stanford's new design school refers to their commitment to the multi-disciplinary, highly interactive community approach they foster. Says Hasso Plattner, cofounder of software giant SAP and the benefactor who provided $35 million in funding to the school, "Stanford has already proved that students coming from the medical school, the business school, design, engineering, psychology working together for six to nine months on projects, are able to move things forward beyond what any of them could have within their own faculty."[7] ■

packages) decided to introduce pastel-colored plastic revisions of the flashlight! "Everyone" knew that men bought flashlights for their toolboxes. And what man would buy a light green or baby blue or (heaven forbid) pink model? This new product manager had come from the world of dog foods and cereals. She was obviously NOT an expert in flashlights!

Yet, the bold experiment paid off. And very well. Peggy worked with the other members of the sales and marketing team and together they patched together a product-line marketing plan that was a hybrid of traditional flashlight category sales concepts and new consumer packaged goods ideas. Sales skyrocketed in the year after "pastels" were launched. As it turned out, women did buy flashlights. And, multiple colors suggested multiple uses; red for the tool box, blue or pink for the bathroom, green for the kitchen, etc. Instead of buying one flashlight at a time, customers started buying two or even three. The company benefited greatly from the related expertise of a marketer who knew nothing about selling flashlights.

Other Kinds of Related Expertise

Flanders and Cornwell both had deep knowledge of a function that was relevant to the challenge: manufacturing in the case of Flanders, and marketing in the case of Cornwell. But both also brought a naive point of view to the effort because they knew relatively little about the *industry* they joined. (*Note*: Obviously I use the term "industry" loosely in this chapter. There is no SIC [Standard Industrial Classification] code for the flashlight industry, for instance. I simply use the word in reference to the environment in which knowledge is applied. See more information on this in Appendix A.)

But related expertise doesn't have to be based on translating functional knowledge from one industry to another. It can also come simply from having a broad understanding of a particular industry or environment. An engineer from the networking industry, for instance, can bring valuable insights to a marketing team in that same industry without knowing much about marketing—as the following story illustrates.

THE DANISH KING

In 1997 Intel engineering manager Jim Kardach was charged with helping to pull together a Special Interest Group (SIG) to align around a common standard for a wireless networking technology. Technology SIGs, which are composed of many industry players all seeking to agree on a common set of technology parameters so their products can work together, are one of the most common vehicles for bringing new technologies to market. In this case numerous companies, including Intel, Nokia, and Ericsson, had been working on slightly different versions of the same technology, and all had agreed that a single standard would be in the best interest of everyone.

To those who assume that technical considerations are the most contentious and carefully deliberated items on a SIG's agenda, I suggest sitting through an industry-wide discussion regarding what to name a new technology. Counter to their stereotype, engineers can be quite a passionate lot. And the marketers who work for engineering companies (who also frequently have engineering backgrounds themselves) can be even more opinionated.

In the case of what would eventually become Bluetooth, each major company in the SIG already had a proposed name for the technology chosen by its marketing experts. Jim Kardach was no marketing expert. But he did have related expertise as an engineer in the industry. And he had his own idea about what the name should be: the highly unorthodox moniker he had been living with as the technology codename for months—Bluetooth.

Kardach, an avid history buff with definite renaissance tendencies, originally came up with the codename (something every Intel technology has as it is being developed and before marketing assigns it a "real" name) because it was fun and clever. The name was a nod to Harald Bluetooth, the tenth-century Danish king who united Norway, Denmark, and Sweden under Christianity. The technology networked (united) various electronic devices, many of which were telecommunications oriented. And telecommunications companies were predominantly headquartered in and around Norway, Denmark, and Sweden. Kardach figured that if Bluetooth the King could unite the countries, then Bluetooth the technology could certainly unite the countries' devices.

As Kardach lived with the Bluetooth name he began to think that it had potential as more than a temporary code. He loved that it was original and it didn't sound "techie" like some of the other recent names for technologies—PCMCIA, AGP, and PCI for instance. And he thought the story behind it was interesting and added personality to what the public might otherwise perceive as just another sterile technical advance.

The marketing experts in the SIG however didn't agree. The general consensus among them was that the name was terrible, conjuring images of poor dental hygiene rather than high tech capability. Their conviction (backed by some market research) was that the name was so inappropriate that it would be horribly expensive to establish in the public as being synonymous with a state-of-the-art, wireless networking technology. Some went so far as to suggest the name was embarrassing.

But Kardach was unswayed. Over time he converted one influential marketing ally, Intel's Simon Ellis (who also, by the way, has strong renaissance tendencies), and together they inserted the name Bluetooth into every presentation they made to SIG members—just as a placeholder until the "real" name could be established. Apparently, familiarity didn't breed contempt in this case. With increased exposure to the weird name, the marketing experts started to let down their guard. It grew on them. When, thanks to a series of timing issues and trademark obstacles, the "real" name didn't materialize in time for the SIG's press launch date (something no one wanted to change), the marketing team's disdain for the name had decreased to the level that they agreed to launch with Bluetooth as the temporary name—"temporary" being a key word emphasized in all press releases. The plan was that they would have time to complete their search for a permanent name later.

That "later" never came. The story of the Danish king, the weird visual that the name evoked, and the strange juxtaposition of all this with a breakthrough technology was hugely popular. Kardach had been right. It was unique. It was memorable. And it became a hit. Worldwide press articles ran featuring the odd name and telling the story of Harald Bluetooth. It become so successful in fact, that although it typically takes millions of dollars to establish the meaning of a brand in the public mind, shortly after launch when the SIG requested trademark protection for Bluetooth, it was initially turned down. Why? The U.S. Trademark Office determined that the term was synonymous with wireless networking technology, and was therefore NOT protectable. Go figure. The name that was so inappropriate that the "experts" believed it would take vast resources to establish had been melded into the public psyche unintentionally![9]

Jim Kardach's related expertise as a technology engineer allowed him to see something the industry's marketing experts hadn't: the power of a story and an unexpected name. His persistence eventually won some of those experts over to his side even before his theory was proven. Simon Ellis summed up the value of Kardach's contribution pretty well when he said, "Sometimes the best way to get things done is by not knowing what can't be done."

The Gossamer Condor

One final example of related expertise based on knowledge of an industry, but little functional experience, is the story of Paul MacCready and the Gossamer Condor.

In 1977 the Gossamer Condor, which is now exhibited in the Smithsonian, won the largest cash prize up to that time for excellence in a human-powered plane (Figure 6-1). In the following excerpt from a speech given by Paul MacCready, one of the Condor's developers, he outlined how his lack of functional experience in wing design but broad industry expertise in aeronautics was one of the keys to the team's success:

> I am often asked why did your team win, when all those teams with more people and time and resources produced sophisticated vehicles that did not come close to winning? I gave this question a great deal of thought, and realized that among the several answers is one of great importance. Each other team had a specialist for every discipline, and so the wing structure was constructed starting from conventional

Figure 6-1. The Gossamer Condor. Photo published with permission of Dr. Paul B. MacCready, Jr.

> ➤The general consensus among the marketing experts
>
> was that the name Bluetooth was terrible, conjuring im-
>
> ages of poor dental hygiene rather than high tech capa-
>
> bility ∎

structural design by an excellent structural engineer from the aircraft industry. I have an aerodynamics background that let me set some specifications for how large and light the wing had to be, but I have no background in aircraft wing structure.

Thus, in my naiveté, I started from first principles (with some insights left over from building indoor model airplanes in the 50s and hang gliders in the early 70s), pretended I had never seen an airplane before, and came up with the Gossamer Condor approach that permitted a 96-foot span vehicle to weigh only 55 to 70 lbs. The other engineers also knew about indoor models and hang gliders, but they knew so much about their specialty that an easier approach was not apparent. My naiveté was actually a strength for this pioneering stage of human-powered flight.[10]

MacCready brought a new perspective to the effort because he had a broad view of the industry but was not steeped in the expert thinking associated with the specifics of wing design. Pardon the bad pun, but his related expertise helped the project soar.

• GAINING STEAM •

The idea of related expertise as a way to generate innovative insights is gaining momentum. The book, *The Medicci Effect* by Frans

Johansson, is dedicated to the idea that "new discoveries, world-changing discoveries, will come from the intersections of disciplines, not from within them."[11] And numerous academics have researched and are publishing their findings in this space, including Mark and Barbara Stefik, whose innovation research, published by MIT press, I referred to earlier in this chapter. "When people from different fields come together, new ideas can arise from the collision of their viewpoints," they say.[12]

The groundswell of research in this arena has not escaped the attention of the scientific community. In 2003 for instance, the U.S. National Institutes of Health (NIH) launched a program to proactively orchestrate collisions among disciplines in order to stimulate innovation. The NIH mission is to uncover "new knowledge about the prevention, detection, diagnosis, and treatment of disease and disability, to accelerate both the pace of discovery in these key areas, and the translation of therapies from bench to bedside." In order to achieve that mission, the NIH administration recognizes that it is increasingly dependent on scientific discoveries and advances at the intersection of disciplines. Their research suggests that the traditional *multi*-disciplinary approach to problem-solving, in which people from different disciplines work together, should be supplemented with an *inter*-disciplinary approach in which one person is trained or immersed in multiple disciplines.

The effort they launched awards funding to academic institutions who promote inter-disciplinary training. Two types of programs targeted at undergraduate, graduate, or post-doctoral students are eligible.

The first are *Short Lab Courses*. These courses immerse students from one discipline, such as mathematics, into another discipline, such as human biology over a 3- to 8-week period, with the goal being simply to stimulate open-ended new ideas among the participants. The second type of program is called a *Short-Term Research Institute*. These 8- to 10-week sessions immerse students from various disciplines in a specific research problem. The objective in this case is for the students to apply what they know to what they are learning in order to come up with innovative ideas to solve a specific problem.

In both cases these programs are aimed at integrating one discipline with another. But the NIH isn't focused on those students who are likely to be completely naive in the sciences. It is looking for students with promising related expertise. In particular, they encourage institutions that are interested in competing for funding to focus on programs that integrate math and physical, behavioral, and social sciences with traditional biomedical sciences.[13]

The evidence mounts:

Naiveté + a potential-intersection point = a powerful combination.

• IT'S ALL RELATIVE •

An obvious question I often get is, "What kind of related expertise should I look for in a Zero-Gravity Thinker?" My response is that I'm not convinced there is a definitive answer to that question (though it is one I continue to explore). It depends on the nature of the problem, the make-up of the team, the personality and overall characteristics of the Zero-Gravity-Thinker candidate, the time-frame available, and critically, the role you need filled. More on this topic in Chapter 7.

Appendix A suggests one framework for thinking about relevant related expertise for a project. But it is not necessarily the right framework for every situation. In the end, it might be best not to over-think the concept. The idea, after all, is to insert a perspective that will lead to unanticipated insights. For most efforts, a highly creative outsider who is "smart-enough-to-understand-the-basics" is probably a sufficient criterion.

A way to capitalize on naiveté is to find people who aren't working in the same industry or occupation, but have expertise in another area that allows them to see your problems—and possibly solve them—from a new perspective.[14] — *Professor Robert Sutton, Stanford University*

• KEY POINTS •

I. Seeing a challenge through the eyes of someone who is naive can generate unexpected and valuable insights.

2. Related experts are naive in some aspects of a challenge, but are expert in a field or discipline that is adjacent or relevant to it.

3. The related expert who is "smart-enough-to-understand-the-basics" can stimulate a team of experts to think about a challenge from the "beginner's perspective" while also introducing insights from another field.

PART III

. . . .

DEFYING GRAVITY

Theory is splendid, but until put into practice it is valueless. — *James Cash Penney, founder of JC Penney Department Stores*

Part III of this book addresses the "how to" of overcoming the burden of what we know.

Chapter 7 outlines the roles a Zero-Gravity Thinker can play, with particular emphasis on the underutilized but highly powerful Collaborate role. Chapter 8 provides guidance for when to engage and where to find a Zero-Gravity Thinker to play this role, and Chapter 9 gives practical advice for working with outsiders in this capacity.

Chapter 10 is the do-it-yourself section. Even without Zero-Gravity Thinkers, teams can improve their innovation quotient (IQ) by using these techniques. And Chapter 11, the final chapter, addresses the crucial responsibility of the leader in stimulating innovative thinking and making Zero-Gravity-Thinker engagements successful.

Finally, as convenient as it would be to have a one-size-fits-all set of rules to follow, there isn't one. Consider the advice noted in this book as a starting point. Innovate from there.

CHAPTER 7

THE COLLABORATOR

WHAT DOES A ZERO-GRAVITY THINKER ACTUALLY DO?

Collaborations increase the speed of innovation. —
National Innovation Initiative[1]

EGGS MAY BE THE MOST versatile food on the planet.
Whip them into meringue and they add a tasty and visually appealing finishing touch to desserts. Fry them, boil them, poach them,
scramble them and they are a perfectly satisfactory stand-alone
entrée. Or, in perhaps their most powerful role, mix them into
batter as an ingredient and they turn something that might have
been good into something far better. Cakes stand taller and have
more structure. Cookies are moister. For such a small package,
there is an awful lot of potential inside—depending on how the
cook decides to use it.

Though Zero-Gravity Thinkers are not as interchangeable as
eggs—renaissance tendencies are the only characteristic that stays
constant; psychological distance and related expertise are specific

to a group and challenge—they are a lot like eggs in one respect: They have the potential to make a significant impact. But the degree of impact they can make and the direction that impact is likely to take are entirely dependent on how the team decides to use them and on the role they are asked to play.

• OUTSIDE ROLES •

There are five roles outsiders (with or without Zero-Gravity Thinker characteristics) can play on a team. They fall into two categories: 1) the *Process* category, which focuses on the "how to" of solving a problem and includes the Teach and Facilitate roles; and 2) the *Content* category, which focuses on actually solving a problem and includes the Inform, Collaborate, and Do roles (Figure 7-1).

Though a Zero-Gravity Thinker can add value in both categories, the focus of this chapter will be on the Content category, with a particular emphasis on the underused Collaborate role. The rationale is that because Process roles are more focused on the "how to" of innovating, they don't take full advantage of what a Zero-Gravity Thinker can contribute in actually solving a specific challenge.[2]

Following is a brief description of all the roles:

Process Roles

Process roles are focused on the methods, behaviors, practices, and skills that enhance the ability of a team to solve a problem. Zero-Gravity Thinkers can be helpful in these roles, but this isn't where teams typically get optimal value from them.

Figure 7-1. Roles outsiders can play.

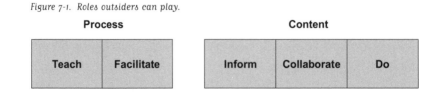

Teach Role

This role is focused on helping a team improve its own ability to innovate by enhancing management practices, creativity skills, culture, etc. The best teachers typically come in the form of highly adept external coaches. But even books and articles can help us learn ways to improve our innovation capabilities. Teachers don't necessarily have to know anything about a specific challenge to help a team improve its capabilities.

Facilitate Role

Facilitators help teams follow a process that will lead to innovative insights related to a challenge. The process might be short and quick, like a brainstorming session, or long and involved, like a months-long strategic planning effort. Think of facilitators as guides. Like teachers, they don't have to actually contribute to solving the problem, they just have to help teams maneuver their way through it.

Content Roles

Content roles are focused on applying experience, knowledge, insights, and imagination to a problem in order to solve it. These are roles in which Zero-Gravity Thinkers can add the greatest value.

Inform Role

When teams want input on a specific challenge, they might try to become better informed by asking for the opinions and insights of outsiders. These outside "counselors" can be customers, allies, fellow-travelers, suppliers, or even other experts who have been given some context in which to offer their thoughts regarding a situation. This type of outside interaction is usually relatively short: a conversation or two, a few hours here or there.

Collaborate Role

This role is highly underutilized, but has the potential to be the most powerful of all roles in helping a team address a specific challenge. When teams employ this role, they ask an outsider to participate deeply with them as both a partner in developing innovative ideas and as a catalyst for stimulating the team to think about a challenge from a different perspective. Because this role is so important and so underused, it will be the focus of much of the latter part of this chapter (Figure 7-2).

Do Role

This role is employed by teams when they don't have the in-house capability they need to address a challenge. In other words, they hire an outsider to "do" what they can't do. Teams, for instance, may ask advertising consultants to deliver ad campaigns, manufacturing firms to deliver finished goods, or software contractors to deliver software code. Though the teams usually provide guidance and input, they rarely participate with the outsider to deliver the advertising, manufacturing, or software coding. It is the outsider who is responsible for the deliverable—and to a large degree, whether or not it is innovative. This role is employed frequently and, as a result, is often the way teams encounter innovative new concepts from outside.

(*Note*: Roles sometimes overlap, and outsiders occasionally play more than one at a time.)

• ZERO-GRAVITY INFORMERS AND DOERS •

Let's zoom in now on the Content category: the Inform, Collaborate, and Do roles. We will, however take them a bit out of order,

Figure 7-2. The Content roles.

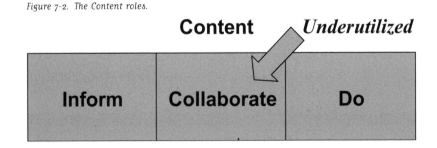

starting with the most common roles: Inform and Do. We'll save the exploration of why the Collaborate role is likely to be so innovation-stimulating but is so underutilized for last.

Quick Takes

The *Inform role* is the most common role outsiders are asked to play. Most of us employ it on a regular basis—though rather informally (pardon the play on words). After all, it's relatively quick and easy to ask for the input and opinion of a supplier, a friend who works in a related field, or even a coworker from another department. From time to time most of us even employ it more purposefully. The Jim Beam Company, for instance, conducts regular working sessions with bar owners and bartenders to stay at the forefront of what young adults are looking for in new drinks.[3] Intel listens to what industry engineers have to say about technology challenges or future opportunities at (among other places) their twice-yearly, worldwide Intel Developer Forums. And most of us conduct focus groups from time to time to hear what potential customers think about everything from new product concepts to the latest ad campaign we're running.

However, when organizations really want to squeeze all of the potential they can from this role they do something a bit differently: They invite in a few Zero-Gravity Thinkers.

Case in point: the U.S. Navy has a Strategic Studies Group (SSG), whose goal is to think about how warfare might be conducted thirty to fifty years from now. The idea is to examine every possible contingency so U.S. armed forces will be better prepared—regardless of what the future holds. The group itself is composed of a small team of highly intelligent, curious Navy personnel. These folks, however, are regularly joined by an eclectic, ever-changing group of outsiders with, you guessed it, Zero-Gravity-Thinker characteristics.

Although SSG interacts with these outsiders in various formats and settings, perhaps one of the most interesting is a three-hour think-session they host on a regular basis with about thirty-five participants. A variety of Zero-Gravity Thinkers, including science fiction authors, academics, economists, handwriting experts, businesspeople, and even musicians have been asked to participate in these think-storms—essentially a smorgasbord of creative outsiders with sometimes only the barest hint of related expertise. What does SSG get out of these efforts? New information, unique opinions, wildly different perspectives, and insightful ideas—exactly what they should be looking for from Zero-Gravity Thinkers playing the Inform role.

Companies like Kraft Foods and Quaker Oats have also discovered the value of Zero-Gravity Thinkers in this role. Working with an ideation firm called ThinkShop, these companies have tapped the insights of creative outsiders to help them develop dozens of new product ideas.

The method ThinkShop uses for its clients employs many of the same elements as other ideation firms. For instance, they conduct their sessions in inspiring locations like beach resorts or art museums and use fun and surprising props like Play Doh® to encourage participants to make their ideas "real."

ThinkShop, however, also throws something a little different into the mix for each assignment—what they call "Outside Experts." Not surprisingly, ThinkShop's Outside Experts (usually between one and three per session) have Zero-Gravity-Thinker characteristics. Armed with a general understanding of the challenge, these outsiders use the power of their fresh perspectives to work side by side with clients to put a new spin on old assumptions. Alone, their ideas might be of limited value, but when combined with those of a highly expert team, they can spark associations that often lead to significant breakthroughs.

These sessions with Zero-Gravity Thinkers in the Inform role are short and intense. But for clients like Quaker Oats and Kraft Foods, they are often the starting point for high-impact innovations.

Zero-Gravity Thinkers *Do* It Better

The other common Content role is the *Do role*. As already noted, this role is employed by teams when they need someone to do

▶**Synectics**

Another example of a consulting group that uses Zero-Gravity Thinkers in facilitation sessions to better "inform" its clients is the innovation consulting firm Synectics. Candis Cook, a principal with the firm, told me recently about their commitment to bringing in people with these characteristics to work with clients. They call these outsiders "Analogous Experts." In one session for an insurance client, who was trying to determine how to stimulate people to buy a relatively unpopular product, the Analogous Experts included a personal trainer and a funeral pre-sale manager. Though both were creative outsiders, their related expertise was particularly interesting. They both had experience in persuading people to do things they weren't inclined to do—even if those things were in their best interest. ■

what they can't do, by teams that lack some critical competency or resource required for getting the job done (Figure 7-3).

Most of us bring outsiders in to play this role for projects on which we need help intermittently. And, a good share of the time, innovation isn't a key goal. But when it is, making sure that these

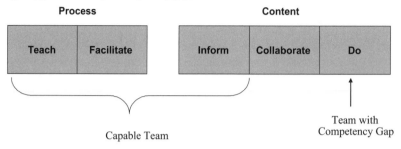

Figure 7-3. The Do role fills competency gaps.

specialized extra arms and legs also have Zero-Gravity-Thinker characteristics can bring huge rewards.

One of the most famous and successful of all companies focused on doing what their clients typically can't is IDEO. Of course, IDEO is renowned for its innovative design capabilities, from the look they created for the Palm V organizer for Palm Computing, to the Shopping Cart Concept that was featured prominently on ABCs *Nightline* a few years ago, to the Crest Neat Squeeze Tubes (the toothpaste tubes that stand up). How does IDEO consistently win awards and accolades for the inventive way it brings value to its clients? Though IDEO's general manager Tom Kelley has written a couple of excellent books outlining the keys to their success, what is particularly relevant to this discussion is the type of people they employ.

IDEO refers to its people as T-shaped: deep in at least one discipline and broad in many others. A recent *BusinessWeek* article refers to them a little differently. It suggests that it is so fun and rewarding to work with IDEO because they tend to hire "polymaths—people with two or three advanced degrees who climb mountains, go birding in the Amazon, and bike through the Alps."[4] I'd put an even different spin on it. I'd say they hire people with Zero-Gravity-Thinker characteristics. And IDEO's employees exemplify the kind of outsiders an organization should be looking for when it wants innovative solutions from those it hires to Do what it can't.

Intel has been the beneficiary of working with such people in this role. And more than once Intel hasn't had to tap into a world-

▶**The T-Shaped People of IDEO**

Craft. Collaboration. Left-brain, right-brain. Passion. Curiosity. These are words that IDEO people use to describe what they have in common with each other. We're not talking about company spirit, but the medium in which good ideas are born and flourish.

People here are T-shaped: broad and deep. Broad in their skills and interests and able to work with a wide range of people. Deep in their knowledge and experience in one or more disciplines. — IDEO website, August 2005 ■

famous firm like IDEO to find them. Several years ago, for instance, the company hired Portland marketing communications consultant Cheryl Vandemore and the team she was heading to create an interactive direct marketing campaign for its networking division. The interesting thing about Vandemore is that she is not only an expert in marketing communications, but she also has strong renaissance tendencies (she's able to connect seemingly disparate concepts into high value ideas faster than most people can speak) and is often able to put that characteristic, as well as psychological distance and some type of related expertise, to work for her clients in a high-octane manner.

Initially Intel's project called for the development of an electronic game that could be mailed on CD-ROM to the IT professionals who manage corporate networks. These LAN (local area network) managers were used to getting pretty serious, dry mailings from Intel about its networking software and adapter cards. And, their response rate to these mailings was, if not low, at least terribly predictable.

But Cheryl had related expertise in marketing rental videos and creating entertaining, out-of-the-ordinary advertising campaigns. And this related expertise (along with her other Zero-Gravity-Thinker characteristics) encouraged her to push Intel down a path very different from the one it was used to taking. Cheryl and her team went beyond a mere game to a storytelling experience. They created an electronic video world called "LANtropolis" and populated it with villains like the Bandwidth Hog, a bloated, animated pig that clogged the city's arteries (network connections), and heroes like Gig Hardrive, a cool 1950s-style detective, who used Intel networking products to overcome the evil bandwidth thief. The resulting mini-movie showcased Intel's products in a way that no one ever had before. When the approximately twelve-minute video-clip was played at the sales conference that year, it stole the show, generating the kind of excitement and enthusiasm that only something brilliantly out of the ordinary can do. And, best of all, customers loved it, responding at nearly twice the rate they did to Intel's more traditional mailings.

Intel's decision to hire a Zero-Gravity Thinker in the Do role for this effort resulted in an innovation that not only pumped up customers, it energized and excited the employee base as well. Even now, years later, there are people at Intel with the LANtropolis "movie" posters still displayed in their offices.

Role Limitations

To recap: Zero-Gravity Thinkers in the Inform and Do roles are a valuable way to insert new thinking into an effort. Nevertheless, teams should recognize that these common outsider roles have limitations in their ability to stimulate innovation.

The biggest drawback of the Inform role is that it is rather superficial. Interaction time with the team is typically limited, and people in this role rarely have deep knowledge of the situation, making their inputs of limited value. The Do role has its own unique drawback. While not superficial, it is frequently confined to the projects or portions of projects a team is incapable of handling itself—efforts, in other words, that are not likely to be considered most critical to the success of an organization. (This isn't to say that challenges that are outsourced are unimportant. It is simply an observation that an organization's core competencies are typically staffed internally.) The point is that Zero-Gravity Thinkers are likely to be only superficially (versus deeply) involved in our most important challenges.

> ▶ Zero-Gravity Thinkers are likely to be only superficially (versus deeply) involved in our most important challenges! ∎

If innovation is the goal, based on what we know about Group-think, ExpertThink, and the Paradox of Expertise, this is backward. It leaves our most critical efforts most vulnerable to the dangers of group thinking, expert thinking, and just plain old stale thinking.

What can we do about this? Implement the underutilized Collaborate role more often (Figure 7-4).

• THE UNDERUTILIZED ROLE •

We can all recall being led to a productive insight by the comment of a colleague who didn't deliver the insight herself but who sparked an association that did the trick.[5] — *Robert Cialdini*

Figure 7-4. The Collaborate role is underutilized because teams without perceived competency gaps rarely bring in outsiders.

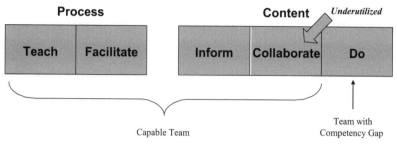

Four characteristics define the Collaborate role and distinguish it from the other roles an outsider can play.

1. Collaborators are deeply immersed in a team and specific challenge—typically over multiple weeks or months—allowing them to get beyond a superficial understanding of the situation. Critically, their focus is on working the problem, not the problem-solving process (though process can certainly be an important part of the effort).

2. Collaborators work with teams that do not have significant competency gaps. Their involvement is meant to augment the innovation efforts of the team's experts, not replace it.

3. The goal of the Collaborator is to deliver or stimulate the team to deliver a more innovative solution than would likely have been developed otherwise. The person in this role does not have to contribute the "big idea" themselves—though they can. If the end result is an innovative solution, then the engagement was successful.

4. Ideally, Collaborators have Zero-Gravity Thinker characteristics, enabling them to challenge Groupthink, disrupt ExpertThink, and fuel imagination during their tenure with the team. Although these characteristics are not crucial for the other roles (though they are highly recommended, particularly for those in the Do role), they should be considered a necessity for this one.

Cynics might condense this definition into something rather unflattering like the following:

> Collaborators are creative people from outside the team who know more about a different industry, function, or discipline than the one being addressed by a highly capable internal team; they are therefore, an unnecessary addition to an effort.

Though I agree that on the surface it might seem a bit wasteful to deeply embed outsiders into a capable team of experts—the key reason, of course, that the role is infrequently utilized—some companies are finding that things are not always as they seem. Read on to find out how some organizations are "wasting" their way to the bank.

Umpqua and Zibites

The Umpqua River flows through southern Oregon and is a favorite destination for outdoor enthusiasts. Originating near Crater Lake, it begins a 250-mile trek through some of the most rugged and beautiful country in the world before it joins the Pacific Ocean near Reedsport, Oregon, home to a whopping population of 4,870 people—at least according to the 2000 census.

Every year scores of kayakers and fly fishermen hike through the trees that stand like sentinels guarding the riverbanks in search of the perfect place to enter the chilly waters. During the summer, adrenaline junkies get their annual fix by whitewater rafting the most treacherous sections of the waterway. What you will find along the Umpqua's path are plenty of opportunities for communing with nature. But what you won't find is much in the way of civilization, big business (unless you count logging), or a particular interest in innovation. Most retail establishments in the towns like Reedsport that dot the Umpqua's path look pretty much the way they did ten, twenty, sometimes even fifty years ago. In some ways, life moves slower along these Main Streets than it does on the laziest portions of the river, which is why this is a strange place for one of the most successful innovation stories in the banking industry to begin.

Our unlikely tale dates back to 1953, when South Umpqua State Bank (the name was later shortened to Umpqua Bank) was founded not far from Reedsport in the tiny town of Canyonville, Oregon, which then had a population of about 900. The bank catered to the loggers and farmers of the region and focused on providing them with friendly, unpretentious customer service. The good and the bad news is that over the years the friendly little community bank was successful and expanded. On the plus side, by 2002 it had just under seventy branches and was no longer confined to communities on the banks of the Umpqua River. Its branches spanned the length of Oregon, from Medford in the south to Portland in the north.

The downside was that expansion had come at a relatively steep price. Following a rather frenzied period of mergers and acquisitions, the organization had become a bit of a hodge-podge. The foundation of Umpqua's success—its friendly, community-oriented culture—was foreign to many of the company's newly acquired employees. And customers who were used to dealing with their various old banks had no idea what to expect from this new one.

Bank president Ray Davis worried that in the competitive world of banking, these early signs of brand dilution might intensify into something far more lethal. So, he decided to nip the problem in the bud. Always a believer in the power of the physical bank environment itself, Davis decided to start addressing the challenge by focusing on creating the "next generation" Umpqua Bank—beginning with the design of its new branch to be opened in Portland.

This wasn't an earth-shattering decision. Many establishments change their physical look when they want to update or strengthen the perception of their brand, and Umpqua had been making the interior atmosphere of what it calls its' stores' an important part of their branding effort for years. Where this story takes a twist, however, is in the way Davis approached this specific challenge. Instead of simply hiring an architectural firm to design an appealing interior environment (as most of us would have), Davis first hired an industrial design firm—one that at the time had far more experience designing objects than spaces people walk through, and, surprisingly, had absolutely no experience in the banking industry. The role Davis wanted this outside firm to play was that of key collaborator. Working with the Umpqua team, this outsider's job would first be to act as a catalyst for fleshing out the true essence of the brand. Then, working with TVA (Thompson, Vaivoda & Associates), the architects who were finally brought in to implement the new design, their task would be to generate insights and ideas that would bridge the bank's brand with its physical environment.

Ziba, the bank-naive collaborator on the project and a rising star in innovation circles, was up for the challenge. The Portland, Oregon-based firm, whose name means "beauty" in Persian, was founded in 1984 by Iranian-born Sohrab Vossoughi. Recently hailed as one of the nation's "Magnificent Seven" top innovation gurus by *BusinessWeek*, Vossoughi is dedicated to building a highly diverse and creative workforce. In fact, when Henry Chin, a Ziba creative director, read the characteristics of Zero-Gravity Thinkers in an e-mail I sent to him before we met, his first thought was, "This is us!"

Whether Ray Davis articulated it or not as he set out to find his collaborative partner for this project, it seems that Ziba's Zero-Gravity-Thinker qualities were precisely what he was looking for: creative outsiders with related but not specific expertise in the banking industry. In fact, Davis later said that hiring a team with banking experience would have been the "kiss of death."

So, Ziba jumped headlong into the effort with stellar results. First, their collaboration with the Umpqua management team crystallized the organization's understanding of its brand and customers. Then, the collaboration with TVA resulted in a host of unique architectural elements that were incorporated into the environment. The effect is an atmosphere inside the branch that is more reminiscent of a hotel lobby or upscale retailer than a bank. Coffee, comfortable chairs, and newspapers that are hung café-style in the sitting area all encourage people to relax and stay for a while—which they do when Umpqua sponsors community events like book readings and knitting clubs. To top it all off, large display panels "productize" the bank's various financial offerings, making them easy to "browse." What customers experience when they step into this Umpqua branch is a feeling of comfortable, unpretentious, community-oriented credibility—exactly the brand positioning Davis wanted to strengthen (Figure 7-5).

All in all the end-result was so impressive that in 2004 Ziba won a prestigious IDEA (Industrial Design Excellence Award) from the Industrial Designers Society of America for its work on the project. The case was also written up by the Design Management Institute and distributed by Harvard Business School Publishing. And, most important, nine months after opening the new Portland branch, Umpqua had exceeded its initial goal of $15 million in new deposits by . . . drum-roll please . . . $20 million, racking up a total of over $35 million in deposits for that period!

Today Umpqua is rolling the brand-strengthening design con-

Figure 7-5. Lobby of Umpqua Bank's Pearl District "store" in Portland, Oregon.

cept out to its other locations, and Ziba is fielding calls from "banks around the world" looking for design assistance, according to director of client relations, Kimberly Curry. But what these banks and others may be missing is the bigger picture. Yes, Ziba played a terrific Collaborate role. And yes, Ziba is staffed with people who are often capable of bringing Zero-Gravity-Thinker characteristics to their clients. But, the key learning here is that inviting the right kind of outsider in to play this seemingly unnecessary role (admit it . . . few of us would have hired Ziba in addition to our internal brand experts or our external architectural firm) can result in enormous innovation benefits.[6]

> Ziba's success stems from "cross-pollination" that occurs when its relatively large staff representing diverse disciplines converges on a project. —*Susan Agre-Kippenhan, chair of Portland State University's art department and professor of design*

From Doing to Collaborating

Umpqua Bank isn't the only company that is benefiting from collaborative efforts with Zero-Gravity Thinkers. Whirlpool (with its Whirlpool, KitchenAid, and Kenmore brands) has an ongoing collaborative working relationship with Ziba's Zero-Gravity Thinkers to develop new design strategies for its products—even though it has hundreds of internal world-class designers. Vossoughi says that their role is increasingly that of a catalyst for bringing together different perspectives both from inside and outside the company to stimulate innovative insights.

Companies like Safeway, Kraft Foods, Kaiser Permanente, and Procter & Gamble are implementing this approach to innovation as well. Perhaps not surprising is the fact that one of the partners they turn to as a source of Zero-Gravity Thinkers is IDEO. Though we just discussed them as a world-class "doer," providing industrial design expertise for clients who don't have that in-house capability, increasingly they also play the Collaborate role: acting as a thought-catalyst for clients who would arguably be capable of addressing the challenge themselves—if only they could see it from a different perspective.

For example, Safeway and Kraft Foods turned to IDEO to better link and improve their inventory management systems. Kaiser Permanente asked the firm for help in improving their customers' overall experience, a project which touched on such non-design-related challenges as finding ways to reduce the anxiety patients feel waiting—half-naked—in an exam room for their doctor to show up.[7] And Procter & Gamble recently entered into a deep collaborative relationship with IDEO to develop new products—a significant departure from less collaborative engagements where design firms have traditionally been limited to devising a new look for products the client's staff has already dreamed up.

According to IDEO's general manager, Tom Kelley, the firm might have once viewed it as a slight to have been described as a great collaborator, but not anymore. "Today," he says, "we more often see ourselves working alongside a client group, influencing their culture, altering their patterns of innovation, and leaving them with new tools to continue the forward momentum. When it becomes difficult to distinguish our contribution from that of our clients, we know we're on the right track."[8]

> This is the value of the collective effort—nobody is really sure who is inventing because, in fact, the inventions emerge in the interactions of the group.[9]
> —Dean Takahashi, author of Opening the Xbox, regarding the team effort to develop the gaming device

Bright Ideas

Industrial design firms are at the forefront of the collaborative Zero-Gravity-Thinker model, perhaps in part because they have embraced the idea of generating high-value, creative collisions between the worlds of form and function for so long. But industrial design firms aren't the only place companies are finding Zero-Gravity Thinkers with which to collaborate. Coca-Cola, Pepperidge Farm, and Georgia Pacific, for example, have all engaged the services of another kind of firm. A company called Brighthouse.

Brighthouse is an Atlanta-based consultancy founded in 1995 by ex-advertising guru, Joey Reiman. Billing itself as "the world's first Ideation Corporation," the company adheres to the belief that true innovation is the result of an organization's interaction with outsiders who can offer relevant and divergent insights.

The Brighthouse process immerses multiple Zero-Gravity Thinkers (they simply call them "Thinkers") in a client's challenge to collaborate with them over a sixteen-week period. Each eclectic working-group consists of Brighthouse's own team as well as outsiders who are referred to as Luminaries. These Luminaries might include world-class artists, professors, business people, government officials, and even specialists in technical fields like nuclear physics, who are chosen to participate based on the specifics of the project. So valued are these interactions with what I would call Zero-Gravity-Thinker teams that clients pay fees of up to $1 million for the resulting insights and ideas.

One specific example of the success of the Brighthouse approach is when they combined forces with fragrance powerhouse Coty, Inc., to search for new product opportunities. For that assignment the Luminaries who participated were well-regarded sociologists who focused on women's trends and issues. These sociologists and the Brighthouse team encouraged the Coty executives to rethink the existing mindset within the fragrance industry (ExpertThink) that suggested women primarily wore perfume to please the man in their life. Instead they proposed that trends in women's attitudes suggested women were becoming more likely to wear fragrances primarily to please themselves.

This mindset challenge, as well as the subsequent dialogue between the Brighthouse team, the Coty team and the sociologists, led to the development of Ghost Myst perfume. Within a year of its introduction this new product became a top-selling fragrance in the United States.[10] Was the money Coty spent on Brighthouse worth it? According to Reiman, the payment he received from Coty was $308,000 or about 1 percent of the $30 million retail revenue Ghost Myst generated that year. I'll leave the value assessment up to you.

Slow Gin

Other companies, perhaps those who can't or don't want to spend a significant amount of money for this type of engagement, are implementing more modest collaborative Zero-Gravity-Thinker efforts (though they are not generally called this). The role I have had at Intel is a good example: a small-scale, relatively inexpensive implementation of the concept. And more options for implementing these efforts are outlined in Chapter 9.

But leaders should be cognizant of one important consideration before moving down this path. The Collaborate role requires something that is sometimes more scarce than money. It requires time.

Research suggests that our need-for-speed is almost as likely to kill innovation as Groupthink and ExpertThink. Dean Keith Simonton is a professor of psychology at the University of California at Davis, who has studied creativity and genius extensively. His work suggests that when people are rushed to solve a problem in a limited time frame their level of arousal increases due to excitement and frustration. This stress constricts thinking, which leads to a focus on high-probability associations, i.e., the combinations of ideas and concepts that are most likely.[11] In other words, speed thwarts our ability to think innovatively. Therefore, before deciding to implement a collaborative Zero-Gravity-Thinker engagement, leaders should be sure they can devote adequate time (think weeks or months versus days) to the effort.

One organization that definitely thinks in long periods of time for innovation work is The Global Innovation Network (GIN). GIN is a business think-tank based in London and Sydney that, like Brighthouse, engages in collaborative roles with Zero-Gravity-

Thinker types to uncover opportunities for organizations in new product development and brand strategy. Their client roster includes companies like Virgin Atlantic Airways (with whom they worked on a project related to gaining a competitive advantage via airline food, of all things!), Toyota, Unilever, and Deutsche Telekom. For them, time is not a luxury, but a necessity as the following excerpt from their website illustrates:

> If you're in a hurry and you want to contact us please don't. We're busy and have enough work. More importantly, if you're in that much of a rush we can't help you (we're interested in things that are important, not things that are urgent).
>
> However, if you'd like to think about the future (and you don't need an answer tomorrow) write to us with your question or explain the nature of your problem (ideally on a single sheet of paper) and we'll write back once we've had time to think about it. — Global Innovation Network website, August 2005

The key takeaway is that it's better to get the input of a Zero-Gravity Thinker through one of the other four roles than try to speed the interaction with one in a Collaborate role. Worse than too little Zero-Gravity-Thinker input are unrealistic expectations for an interaction that is time-starved from the beginning.

• BEING INTUITIVE •

To many of the people I have spoken with on this topic, searching for Zero-Gravity Thinkers to fill the Teach, Inform, Facilitate and Do roles is almost a no-brainer. Many haphazardly do this now, and have simply vowed to be more consistent in this effort moving forward.

The Collaborate role however is more perplexing. Though many acknowledge it makes conceptual sense, they have questions regarding implementation (which will be addressed in the next two chapters) and remain concerned with how they will "quantify" the impact an outsider might have had in delivering the "big idea"—particularly if the outsider did not clearly produce it themselves.

My response is to say that for any single project, perhaps we can't always quantify their contribution—at least not with any great degree of reliability. I realize this will be a rather unpopular point of view with some. However, consider the following story:

In a study conducted by psychologist and creativity researcher Robert Epstein, participants were placed in a room that had two ropes dangling from the ceiling. The ropes were far enough apart that a person couldn't reach one while holding on to the other. The participants were asked to list ways they could connect them. Nearby was a list of objects that could be used, including a pair of pliers. Most respondents had great difficulty in solving the problem until an experimenter gently (but almost imperceptibly) touched one of the ropes so that it swayed slightly. Almost immediately after this, most participants came up with the idea to tie the pliers to the end of one of the ropes creating a sort of pendulum. The participant could then hold one rope and grab the other one as it swung near. The interesting thing about this was that when the participants were asked how they came up with the idea, none of them could articulate it. It just "came to them." None recalled that the rope had moved just prior to their "insight."

Although all of the people in this study had the knowledge they needed to solve this problem (they had no competency gaps), none did solve it until they were stimulated by an outsider's actions. More important for this discussion however, is the fact that none even realized an outsider had been responsible for their "breakthrough." The point? Even when outsiders stimulate insights, we don't necessarily realize it. As much as we may try to measure, quantify, predict and even understand our ability to generate innovative ideas, we frequently remain clueless.

Recall the quote from Albert Einstein that started this book: "The intuitive mind is a sacred gift and the rational mind is a faithful servant. We have created a society that honors the servant and has forgotten the gift." Where innovation is concerned, I propose that we relinquish some of our obsession with what can be exactingly measured and rely more on what makes intuitive sense.

In the short term, failing to utilize the Collaborate role because we aren't confident we will be able to determine whether and how far a particular Zero-Gravity Thinker moved one of the "ropes" that might have led us to an insight seems to be based on the highly dangerous view (at least where human behavior and insight is concerned) that we should only act on what can be measured. Like eggs in the mix, the precise impact Zero-Gravity Thinkers have on an effort may not always be easy to measure, but somehow the collective end result is better when they are included.

➤ A Note on Business Leaders and Intuition

The capacity for making intuitive decisions is a basic ingredient of creativity. Intuition is trusting the vision of the unconscious, letting go of the self-conscious control of the thinking mind. It is so often opposed in the workplace because it can't be measured or quantified or rationally justified. But it has the ring of truth because it is grounded in the ability of the unconscious to organize information into unanticipated new ideas.

Operating a business in the global arena demands innovative ways of understanding and responding . . . businesspeople who know how to listen to their customers rather than just study figures and statistics will have

a splendid future, and those who are able to draw on
their intuition will emerge as natural leaders.[12]
—Daniel Goleman, Ph.D. and Paul Kaufman ∎

• KEY POINTS •

1. There are two categories of roles outsiders can play for a team: Process and Content. Process roles are focused on the "how to" of solving a problem. Content roles are focused on actually solving it.

2. There are two Process roles: Teach and Facilitate. Since these roles are focused on process versus actual problem solving, these roles are not ones in which Zero-Gravity Thinkers add the most value. The three Content roles are: Inform, Collaborate, and Do. These roles benefit greatly from Zero-Gravity Thinker involvement.

3. The Collaborate role is the least commonly deployed but may have the greatest potential for innovation impact. Zero-Gravity Thinkers in these roles act as participating catalysts, participating in the problem-solving process, and stimulating others on the team to "think differently" at the same time.

CHAPTER 8

WHEN AND WHERE . . .

WHEN DO YOU NEED A COLLABORATOR
AND WHERE DO YOU FIND ONE?

A little help at the right time is better than a lot of
help at the wrong time. — *Anonymous*

SINCE COLLABORATIVE efforts require time and the addition of at least one person to the team, they aren't practical for most challenges. But which ones are worth the extra effort?

• WHEN DO YOU NEED A COLLABORATOR? •

One way to decide is to classify the problem into one of three categories: Big Ps, Little Ps, and Exploratories.

Big Ps

Big Ps are Big Picture Problems. They are complex, multi-dimensional, systemic or strategic challenges that affect many functions or actions. Examples include corporate or business group strategy, full product manufacturing processes, complex product design efforts (airplanes, computers, cars), or ecosystem management. Decisions related to Big Ps have long-lasting and far-ranging impacts.

When Intel decided, for instance, that the way to achieve future growth was to shift its corporate strategy away from focusing on single-benefit-technologies (like fast microprocessors) to technologies that could be combined in multiple-benefit-platforms (like fast microprocessors + wireless networking capability, such as the Centrino chipset), they were implementing a solution to a Big P problem, "How do we keep our core product from becoming a commodity?" That solution had a significant impact on virtually every facet of the organization.

Similarly, when Toyota decided that its electric/gasoline hybrid car, Prius, would operate with a power split device allowing it to run on gas, electricity, or a combination of both at the same time, this was another solution to a Big P problem, "What is the best way to design a hybrid car for a balance of fuel efficiency and performance?" This decision had numerous implications for other components within the car's system: the type of transmission required; the lack of need for a starter; the way the generator, differential, and motor needed to be connected; and so forth—just another example of the vast reach of Big P problems.

Following are the four most common types of Big P problems. Note that frequently they are not distinct but interrelated with one another.

Most Common Types of Big P Problems

1. Strategic direction setting
2. New opportunity identification
3. Competitive or market threat reaction
4. Complex problem resolution

Although these problems represent only a small fraction of the challenges most teams encounter on a regular basis, they are critical. Consequently, they deserve an enormous amount of our attention and creative energy, and almost always warrant the inclusion of a Zero-Gravity-Thinking collaborator in the process.

Little Ps

The vast majority of challenges most of us encounter however, are Little Ps, or Little Picture Problems. They may be just as hard to solve and require just as much knowledge, strategic thinking skill, and creative capability as Big P problems, but typically they are bounded within the confines of Big P decisions.

For instance, when McDonald's asks an agency to pitch them ideas for a new sales promotion to increase Big Mac purchases under the umbrella of an already established advertising campaign, this is a Little P problem. If the Prius engineering team were asked to reduce the cost of the Prius transmission, they would need to do so within the confines of the Big P power split decision. This, again, is a Little P problem. Even a janitorial team, when asked to decrease the amount of time it takes to clean a building, might need to do so within the parameters established by a broader decision regarding which floors or rooms have to be kept at a certain level of cleanliness.

Most Little P challenges need to be addressed rather quickly and are not terribly crucial or complex. Only a handful of Little P problems are sufficiently challenging and important to warrant the extra time and resources required for the Collaborate role.

Exploratories

The third type of problem is an Exploratory. In fact, calling it a problem or challenge isn't really accurate. Exploratories are just that: explorations of "what ifs." Typically undertaken by think-tanks and R&D organizations, Exploratories start with a question that really doesn't have to be answered, but might be valuable if it were. For most organizations, Exploratories are rare, confined to a small team (if, in fact, they are pursued at all). But for a handful of organizations they represent the sole *raison d'etre*.

The Santa Fe Institute (SFI), for instance, is a highly regarded scientific think-tank, founded in 1984 as a research community "transcending the usual boundaries of science to explore the frontiers of knowledge."[1] Their philosophy is to bring together scientists from a broad range of fields to collaborate on complex problem solving. And they work with and provide insights to a veritable who's who of business partners.

Most of their work, however, could be categorized as highly exploratory. In early 2004, for instance, the institute sponsored a workshop for biologists, paleontologists, technologists, and economists to explore the intersection between biological evolution and technical invention/innovation. The result was published in *Science* Magazine and concluded that the parallels between biology and technology, where invention and innovation are concerned, are a potentially fertile ground for further exploration.[2] That's a provocative thought, but not one likely to yield economic value in the near-term.

Exploratories, always (really, I can think of no exceptions) benefit from the Collaborate role. In fact, the more Zero-Gravity Thinkers on board the better, since breakthrough thinking is the goal, and time is typically not a factor.

Figure 8-1 gives a brief overview of when to utilize the Collaborate role based on the type of challenge being addressed. Note that there isn't a precise demarcation point between one type of problem and another. In particular, the difference between Big P and Little P problems is sometimes quite nebulous. Still, considering where a challenge falls along the spectrum is a helpful starting point in addressing it. The idea is that if the challenge is big, complex, important, and likely to have a significant "trickle down" effect on other areas of the business, then it probably warrants the type of innovative thinking effort that the Collaborate role helps stimulate. Leaders should be cautious, however, not to fall into the trap of assuming a challenge is narrower than it actually is (assuming a Big P is actually a Little P). That mistake can be quite damaging as the following story illustrates.

Type of Problem	Typical Frequency	When to Utilize the "Collaborate" Role
Big P (Broad impact across multiple functions, processes, etc; sets direction for addressing Little P problems.)	Infrequent. Small percentage of challenges most groups face.	Almost always.
Little P (Limited impact outside of primary focus area; must be addressed within parameters of Big P decisions.)	Very frequent. High percentage of challenges most groups face.	Infrequently. Only for most important and complex challenges.
Exploratory (What if questions.)	For most organizations extremely infrequent.	Always.

Senior managers at a large U.S. company were focused on trying to increase the number of African Americans they employed. Convinced that recruiting was the problem, they generated some highly creative and successful ideas for bringing more minorities into their organization. Unfortunately, at the end of several years, they had the same percentage of African Americans in the workforce as when they started. Why? They were tackling the wrong issue (or at least solving only a small part of it).

The problem wasn't that they couldn't attract African Americans to the company. It was that they couldn't retain them once they were there. The company was a revolving door, with minority recruits leaving as quickly as they came in. Why? The African American employees felt isolated—not so much at work, but in their personal lives. Because the firm's offices were located in a predominantly white suburb, there were virtually no minorities in the neighborhoods, schools, or social networks. One African-American employee said in his exit interview that he was tired of having to drive twenty miles to even see someone else who looked like him—aside from the few other African Americans he encountered in the office.

This company was trying to solve a Little P problem ("How do we recruit more African Americans?") when they should first have understood the Big P Problem ("What are all of the reasons the percentage of African American employees is so low at our company?"). The result was not only frustrating and expensive for the organization, but it was potentially damaging to the company's long-term commitment to diversity; in the end, it looked like their institution was not a place where African Americans wanted to stay.

Some of the problem-definition techniques outlined in Chapter 10 can help teams establish a sound problem definition from the start.

• WHERE DO YOU FIND A COLLABORATOR? •

"OK," said a friend of mine after a speech I had given, "let's say I want to 'fight off the innovation killer and defy gravity' by introducing a Zero-Gravity Thinker in the Collaborate role. Where do I find these people? Aren't folks with a combination of psychological distance from my team, renaissance tendencies, and relevant related expertise pretty rare?"

"There are more of them around than you might think," I replied. "The trick is simply to look for creative outsiders who are 'smart-enough-to-understand-the-basics' of your challenge. Said that way it doesn't sound so hard, does it?"

I paused. "Actually, there is one other characteristic you should look for that I haven't mentioned yet—an important but secondary attribute these people should have. Leadership and coaching skills. In other words, they should have enough personal charisma and credibility to provide guidance when necessary, enough people smarts to stand back and let the team (or someone else on the team) drive the effort when appropriate, and the ability to be phenomenal listeners."

"Even with that additional qualification, however, there are multiple sources of collaborators in every industry and function. You just have to look for them."

Following are three of the most common sources of collaborators:

1. Consultants
2. Other groups within your company
3. Loaners from other organizations

Consultants

The consulting community is full of Zero-Gravity Thinkers. Many have broad experience across multiple industries, and the good ones tend to be quick studies. They are also relatively easy to find and are available for short-term projects.

We've already discussed (in Chapter 7) firms like Ziba, IDEO, and Brighthouse, but there are numerous others—sometimes where you don't even expect them. For instance, the chairman of Bain & Company—one of the top management consulting firms in the world, and one noted for being more analytical than creative in its approach—credits much of her success to bringing what I would describe as Zero-Gravity Thinker characteristics to her client projects. In the book *The Medicci Effect*, Orit Gadiesh explains to author Frans Johansson that she coined the term "expert generalist" to describe consultants like her at Bain who, rather than focusing on just one industry, actively seek to transfer their learnings across and among multiple industries. She believes this ability to bring related expertise to her clients has been one of the keys to her success. The other is her passion for learning (renaissance tendencies). Gadiesh proudly claims she reads over 100 books every year—none of which have anything to do with business.[3]

And sometimes we find these people in our own backyards. Consider the help that Intel's Digital Health Group (DHG), which is tasked with exploring ways in which technology can be beneficial in health care, got from a local consultant who had Zero-Gravity-Thinker characteristics.

The situation was that DHG wanted to communicate several new product ideas to potential customers and then gather their feedback to determine whether any of the concepts should be pursued further. A typical market research session of this type might involve some prototypes, a few pictures, and lots of back and forth dialogue between the participants and the facilitator. The problem was that the benefits of futuristic technologies are often difficult to envision. As a result, previous new concept discussions with target audiences had been somewhat disappointing for the Digital Health team. Audiences hadn't been able to grasp how a technology or product might actual fit into their lives based on an illustration or a Styrofoam prototype. Because DHG needed to think of a different way to communicate their ideas to people, they decided to take a risk and look for someone a little different from the typical market research facilitator to help them.

Enter consultant Karen Howells. Karen is a skilled communications and business management consultant, but she is also highly creative and has related expertise in theater (related because theater is also about communicating with an audience). In other words, she had relevant Zero-Gravity-Thinker characteristics for this challenge.

The solution Karen's participation sparked was truly innovative for Intel. Her inspiration led the team to augment the use of prototypes and illustrations of new product concepts with short vignettes showing actors actually using the products. For example, the team carefully crafted a script that dramatized what it would be like for an elderly person living alone to be watching television and have an "It's time to take your medicine" message pop up. They developed another that portrayed a situation in which a "smart" lamp in an elderly person's home came on when their next-door-neighbor was leaving to go for a walk . . . and would welcome company. The mini-dramas brought rather nebulous technologies to life and allowed participants to respond more appropriately to the positives and negatives of each concept.

In the end, the feedback from these "focus troupes" was an important contributor to Intel's recently expanded Digital Health

Group. Several of the concepts are now in various stages of exploration and development. The point? Consultants are a great source of Zero-Gravity Thinkers—and they aren't that rare a commodity if you are brave enough to seek them out.

Other Groups in Your Company

Teams within large organizations that don't have the resources or inclination to fill collaborative roles from outside the company might be able to source a candidate from another internal group. This is essentially how my Zero-Gravity-Thinker engagements for Intel worked. Different groups "borrowed" me for several months at a time, with the "borrowing" group compensating my home group for my employee costs during that period.

On the plus side, this is likely to be a less expensive alternative than hiring a consultant from outside. And, sometimes a pseudo-insider's knowledge of the larger organization is a helpful type of related expertise (see following caution). The challenge, of course, is finding:

1. Someone who is outside the direct project team and political hierarchy with appropriate Zero-Gravity-Thinker characteristics for the team's challenge.
2. An internal group that is willing to let one of their employees allocate a significant amount of time to another group's effort.

One informal way to handle this is to talk to other groups about the type of temporary assignment you have in mind (make sure your audience understands the basic concept of Zero-Gravity Thinkers and the role you want this person to play) and see whether they are open to loaning one of their employees to your team for a while with the understanding that the favor will be returned later. Another option to consider is that some projects can be good short-term engagements for senior people with the appropriate Zero-Gravity-Thinker characteristics who want to hop off of the management track for a bit or perhaps even scale back to part-time work. The nature of the role requires skills and capabilities that often come with years of experience, yet the role itself can often be effective in a less-than-forty-hour week. It is also a role that ends after several weeks or months, which prevents the task-creep that so often turns senior level part-time positions into full-time jobs with part-time pay.

A more formal approach is one taken by Steelcase. Their process identifies and then places their most promising employees temporarily into what senior vice president and chief administration officer Nancy Hickey calls "smart nonexpert" roles. Hickey explained to me that this program does two things. For one, it helps expand the knowledge of the high-potential employee. But importantly, it also introduces a new perspective into the challenges an existing "expert" team is facing. This, as much as the company's innovation lab where diverse work teams gather around the shuffleboard table to think and unwind, is a key part of Steelcase's innovation strategy, and one of the reasons the innovative office environments and furnishings they produce continue to win worldwide awards and recognition.

A slightly different approach is taken by the world's largest software company. "Smart Dummies." That's what a friend of mine told me Microsoft calls the Zero-Gravity-Thinker types from inside the company that help teams think innovatively. John Manferdelli, general manager of Microsoft's Office of the Chief Technology Officer and the head of the company's new business incubation group, hadn't heard that term before. But he did confirm that they try to stimulate innovative thinking by temporarily inserting people into teams who are both "smart in another discipline" and willing to look at things from different and interesting perspectives—people who have Zero-Gravity-Thinker characteristics, in other words.

Sometimes these people come from within the Microsoft labs and stay "on-loan" to a group for an extended period of time. Other times, they are high-caliber graduate student interns who are willing to question the status quo at Microsoft for a few months before returning to their studies. In either case, Manferdelli points out that these people are rewarded not for efficiency, which he says is the way most of us in the business world get our pats on the back, but for creativity and divergent thinking. These people join teams explicitly to stir things up and that, he says, helps fight the innovation-stifling effects of "over-expertise."

> ►**A Caution About Zero-Gravity Thinkers from**
>
> **Internal Sources**
>
> Zero-Gravity Thinkers who come from within an organi-
>
> zation might have some organizational ExpertThink
>
> baggage that a complete outsider won't have. Look for
>
> someone who has proved they aren't afraid to buck the
>
> system a bit. And for goodness sake, don't expect any-
>
> one to play this role for you if they are within your report-
>
> ing structure! ■

The bottom line is that there are numerous options for implementing internal collaboration efforts with Zero-Gravity Thinkers. The key is creativity, flexibility, and a willingness to try different options to find what works best in your organization and culture.

Last But Not Least: Zero-Gravity Thinkers on Loan

Regardless of the size of your organization, for those who don't want to or can't hire a consultant, I have one other suggestion for sourcing a collaborative Zero-Gravity Thinker. Why not arrange a swap program with another company? Why doesn't Nike invite someone from HP manufacturing to act as a Zero-Gravity Thinker in their manufacturing facilities for a few months? Why doesn't Dell invite someone from Adidas' shoe design group to join their PC design team for a while? What would happen if someone from

Starbucks' marketing team joined Amazon's marketing team to play this role? What kind of innovative ideas might my neighbor, who owns several Godfather's Pizza franchises, be introduced to if the manager of a local Blockbuster Video joined his team temporarily?

Yes, of course, some swaps would be impossible for competitive reasons (most problematic would be swaps within the same industry), but many would be possible and could be potentially innovation-provoking for both companies involved. The person playing the Zero-Gravity-Thinker role could first stir things up in their foster company and then bring back new ideas and insights from that experience to their home company.

In fact, the "swap" approach is being advocated in the educational and research communities. In a 2005 research report from a joint committee of the National Academy of Sciences, National Academy of Engineering, and Institute of Medicine of the National Academies, the value of temporary, deep collaborations across different disciplines is highlighted. "We have found," says Diana Rhoten, program officer of the Social Science Research Council, "that full-time, long-term collaborations are not always that effective. They reduce interaction, and they reduce innovation. We need to think about establishing long-term organizational structures that allow for short-term and intensive collaboration experiences intermittently over time."[4]

> ➤ We need to think about establishing long-term organizational structures that allow for short-term and intensive collaboration experiences intermittently over time. — Diana Rhoten ■

The report notes that one place short-term, intensive collaborations are successful is in Japan's National Institute for Advanced

Interdisciplinary Research. The institute, which was founded in 1993, focuses on advanced research in areas such as nanotechnology, optoelectronics (optical memory), and bionic (organic tissue + machine) design. One of the keys to their success has been their dedication to bringing together scientists with expertise in diverse disciplines. Just as notable, however, has been the commitment to making most of those diverse collaborations temporary. Critically almost all of their staff join the institute for short periods of time on loan (or, on swap) from the private sector, universities, or foreign research centers.[5] The report advocates the development of similar models for temporary cross-disciplinary immersion within the U.S. university system as a way to spark innovation and further the advancement of science.

• A FINAL WORD •

People who can play collaborative Zero-Gravity-Thinker roles for us are in abundant supply. The biggest challenge in finding them may simply be that we don't look for or structure an environment that makes room for them. Our traditional roles and our traditional alliance to one organization or one team for a prolonged period of time may be the product of habits and mindsets that are in need of re-examination. It's time to get innovative about the way we cultivate innovation.

▶Edison's Internal Swaps

Thomas Edison seems to have recognized the value of inserting smart employees from one function into another. In the late 1880s he asked Reginald Fessenden, a young electrical scientist in his company, to become a chemist. What precipitated the request was Edison's frustration that none of his existing chemists had been able to produce a flexible material to insulate electric wires. Though Fessenden had no chemistry background, Edison reportedly told him, "I've had a lot of chemists . . . but none of them get results." Fessenden undertook the challenge, studied chemistry, and so impressed Edison that he remained with the chemistry team as their chief chemist.[6] ■

• KEY POINTS •

1. There are three types of challenges: Big P (Big Picture Problems), Little P (Little Picture Problems), and Exploratories (Exploratory Problems).

2. Little Ps, which make up the vast majority of challenges an organization faces, typically aren't worth the time and effort required to employ a Zero-Gravity Thinker in the Collaborate role. Conversely, Big Ps and Exploratories will almost always benefit from the inclusion of a person in this capacity.

3. Potential Zero-Gravity Thinkers are everywhere. Consultants or other groups within large organizations are good potential sources of people with these characteristics. Groups might also be able to source Zero-Gravity-Thinker candidates by temporarily "swapping" employees with a different company.

CHAPTER 9

HOW TO WORK WITH A ZERO-GRAVITY THINKER

ELEVEN QUESTIONS AND ANSWERS

The world hates change, yet it is the only thing that has brought progress. — *C.F. Kettering*

THIS CHAPTER PROVIDES DETAILS of how to work with a Zero-Gravity Thinker (particularly in a Collaborate role) by answering eleven of the most common questions about the human relations- and process-side of things.

Question 1: Is a Zero-Gravity Thinker in the Collaborate role (or any other role) one person, a group of people, or an organization?

Answer: A Zero-Gravity Thinker is a person. Because it is difficult to find someone with an equally strong combination of each characteristic (psychological distance, renaissance tendencies, and relevant related expertise), some teams may choose to bring in more than one Zero-Gravity Thinker to "round things out"—though even working with one less-than-perfect Zero-Gravity Thinker is far better than working with none! This is one of the reasons Brighthouse, the Global Innovation Network, and ThinkShop, three companies that were highlighted in Chapter 7, tend to engage multiple Zero-Gravity Thinkers in their efforts for clients.

Additionally, some organizations, like Ziba, which was also discussed in Chapter 7, have cultures that attract people with Zero-Gravity-Thinker characteristics. The organizations are "Zero-Gravity Thinker" friendly and are likely to deliver highly innovative work, but it is the individuals within the organization who are likely to be Zero-Gravity Thinkers—not the organization itself.

Question 2: Don't team members feel threatened by a Zero-Gravity Thinker asked to play a Collaborate role?

Answer: They certainly can feel threatened. And, if this happens, it can stop innovative thinking before it even begins. After all, a requirement for success is that the Zero-Gravity Thinker and the team work together.

Leaders can do two things to make sure resentment doesn't become an issue:

First, before anyone is hired to play a Collaborate role, leaders must make sure their teams understand the concept, the temporary nature of the role, and the rationale behind it. Critically, the team must realize that adding this role to the mix is a positive way to stimulate innovative thinking, not a punishment for poor performance.

Second, team members need to buy into working with a person in this role. If they don't, the effort will almost certainly fail. After all, collaboration means working together! With this in mind, team members should not only agree to work with a Zero-Gravity Thinker, they should have a say in who the Zero-Gravity Thinker is. This means that, as much as possible, leaders are advised to include team members in the selection process for this person.

Finally, as result of acting in collaborative Zero-Gravity-Thinker roles, I have found that one of the best ways to kick off an assignment is to have a one-on-one conversation with every team member, and share a document similar to the guiding principle of the Zero-Gravity Thinkers shown in the following example.

▶ The Guiding Principles of the Zero-Gravity Thinker

I am not an expert in your business. You and your team are the experts in your business. My job is to use my expertise in a related area to think about and help your team think about challenges or opportunities you are facing in a different way.

I will ask basic questions that you (or others) might think I should know the answer to. Sometimes I might know the answer (or some version of it). Sometimes I might not. What is critical is that I want to hear what the person I'm asking thinks. Research shows that foundational questions help the questionee as much as the questioner, by forcing them to consider the challenge from a different (often naive) perspective.

I can only help the team if its members are open to trying new methods, testing basic assumptions, and looking at the challenge from a different perspective.

Many times the approach I use will not be immediately helpful (sometimes it won't be helpful at all), but the cumulative effect is likely to be a higher level of innovative thinking than would have resulted otherwise.

Our interaction is successful if the team develops a more innovative, high-value solution to the challenge or opportunity it faces than it would have without my involvement. I may come up with the "big idea," but it's even more likely that someone else on the team will. It doesn't matter. In the end, if meaningful innovative thinking and actions result, the effort is a win for everyone. ∎

Question 3: Is the Collaborate role one of a leader or a follower?

Answer: Although people playing this role have to have leadership qualities, the way they exercise them depends on the needs of the team. In most of the collaborative projects in which I've participated I vacillated between playing a participant and a leadership role, depending on the ebbs and flows of the project and the team. Perhaps the critical consideration is "what is required in order to stimulate innovative thinking?" For some teams this may mean the outsider taking a highly explicit leadership role, such as assigning deliverables, setting schedules, or introducing exercises and techniques. For other teams this may mean practicing the gentle art of persuasion behind the scenes. The astute Zero-Gravity Thinker will assess the needs of the team and act accordingly to help them explore innovative options and then converge on one that can be implemented.

Question 4: Is there a specific process for stimulating innovative thinking during the collaborative effort?

Answer: It seems that there are as many processes geared toward stimulating innovative thinking and breakthrough insights as there are people. Many have strong merits. Therefore, rather than stating that any one is always better than another, I submit that circumstances and the players involved dictate which *specific* approach will work best.

Having said this, there are five stages in problem-solving/innovation-development that are fairly universal and worth discussing. Though they may go by different names and be combined together in slightly different ways, these represent the fundamentals of a solid innovative problem solving process (whether working with a Zero-Gravity Thinker or not). As much as possible, these are steps I try to build into projects I work on. The rather un-catchy acronym, DIGI-MIR, is a helpful way to remember them.

DIGI-MIR

➤ *Define:* The period in which the problem (or opportunity) is initially defined. This typically occurs before the decision to hire a collaborative Zero-Gravity Thinker is made, and is often refined or reframed once he or she is on board.

➤ *Immerse:* The period when a Zero-Gravity Thinker begins engaging deeply with the team, researching the challenge and refining the client's initial problem statement.

➤ *Generate:* The period when the Zero-Gravity Thinker and the team begin hypothesizing, developing ideas, modeling, and gathering more information related to potential solutions to the challenge.

➤ *Incubate:* The period when the Zero-Gravity Thinker and team set aside the challenge to allow ideas to percolate and "ripen."

➤*Make It Real*: The period when the Zero-Gravity Thinker and team develop an action plan for implementing the idea.

Note that the references to Zero-Gravity Thinkers during the following detailed discussion of these stages are primarily relevant to the Collaborate role.

Question 5: How long does each stage last?

Answer: It depends on the project, the team, the Zero-Gravity Thinker, the time frame available, and so forth. The situation might dictate spending more time on one stage than another. This is a topic for discussion between the team and the Zero-Gravity Thinker. At any rate, the total time frame for all phases can vary from a few weeks to many months.

What leaders should keep in mind as far as the Collaborate role is concerned is that the outsider needs to be around long enough to add value (remember that they need enough time to get up to speed on the challenge since they are related not specific experts) but not so long that they lose psychological distance. For projects that are on the longer side (multiple months), the Zero-Gravity Thinker can help maintain that distance by steering clear of the "norms" of the team, such as keeping slightly different hours, maintaining a separate office, or declining to participate in most office parties and gatherings. This isn't meant to be antisocial. And, it is fine for a Zero-Gravity Thinker to participate in some camaraderie-building (refer back to the importance of building one-on-one relationships in Question #2). But maintaining some distance is a reminder to everyone involved that the value the Zero-Gravity Thinker brings is as an outsider; not as a regular member of the team. It does no good if the Zero-Gravity Thinker begins falling prey to Groupthink and ExpertThink.

Question 6: What happens in the Definition stage?

Answer: Correctly defining the problem may be the most important part of the innovation effort. Albert Einstein was once asked what he would do if he were told that a comet would hit and destroy the Earth in one hour. He responded that he would spend 55 minutes figuring out how to formulate the question and 5 minutes solving it.[1] Einstein knew, as do many in the field of innovation and strategy development, that the most important step in solving a problem, particularly a problem that requires an innovative solution, is to define it. Yet most managers spend a paltry amount of time on this vital aspect of the innovation process.

Ideally the problem-definition stage is at least a two-part exercise. Part one may take place before a team even determines whether the collaborative role is appropriate. During this time frame, the team (or its leader) develops an initial definition of the problem. They may even work with an outside firm in a facilitating role to help them better define the challenge. Based on the resulting definition, the team can categorize the problem as a Big P, Little P, or Exploratory, and decide whether (and in what capacity) to involve a Zero-Gravity Thinker. The initial problem definition and categorization also helps determine the type of related expertise it might be beneficial for a Zero-Gravity Thinker to have.

Chapter 10 provides some suggestions for better problem definition (getting to the root of the problem), either initially or as part of a reframing effort.

Part two of the problem-definition stage takes place after the Zero-Gravity Thinker has been brought on board. Based on the outsider's assessment of (and immersion in) the challenge, the problem definition may be refined or reframed. Teams should be very open to this revision effort. Often, as the Einstein story suggests, problem definition is the key to an innovative solution and can, therefore, be worth revisiting through the fresh eyes of an outsider.

Question 7: Explain Immersion.

Answer: There are two aspects to the Immersion stage. The first is immersion in the challenge. This is the time for a Zero-Gravity Thinker to become educated in the challenge by deeply reviewing research on the topic, becoming familiar with the team's previous plans and activities, and discussing various aspects of the problem with anyone who is remotely close to it. No question is stupid or off limits. On highly complex projects, this stage can last several very intense weeks (or longer). Teams should be prepared for a lot of questions and no answers during this period.

My personal experience is that when I start a project I often read dozens of documents from multiple sources related to a situation, industry, product, or market. And I frequently supplement that with hour-long (or even multiple hour-long) discussions with many key team members in those first weeks as well—all in an effort to immerse myself as deeply as possible as quickly as possible in the challenge. Some Zero-Gravity Thinkers may even use this time to conduct direct customer research, depending on the challenge and the budget for the project.

The second aspect is immersion in the team. This is the time when Zero-Gravity Thinkers begin to establish a rapport and credibility with the other members of the group. As noted earlier, active listening and a desire to understand the perspectives and concerns of the team are crucial during this time frame. Zero-Gravity Thinkers should not be concerned with impressing the team with their knowledge (they are not, after all, experts in the subject-matter), but should be focused on earning credibility as a thoughtful participant who values the input of each team member. People are more likely to be influenced by someone they like and respect.

Later, when Zero-Gravity Thinkers may be in the difficult position of trying to influence a team's mindset, the credibility and personal connections they established in their first weeks can be the key to a successful engagement.

Question 8: What's the most important thing to keep in mind about Generation?

Answer: Though there is currently debate on this issue, I continue to maintain that a key lesson for anyone who wants to develop more innovative ideas is to focus on developing a lot of ideas.

Thomas Edison set a quota for himself to come up with a minor invention every ten days and a major one every six months. He held 1,093 patents (though we know some were collaborations with employees). Were some of those ideas bad? Undoubtedly a lot of them were. But nestled in among some of the duds were the light bulb and the phonograph. Even if the other 1,091 patents never contributed to anything significant (something that isn't the case), those two alone would have been worth the effort.

What I mean by developing more ideas, however, is not that there need to be dozens of undirected ideas for every challenge. What I mean is that each person on the team needs to become an "idea-person"—someone who practices coming up with ideas and voicing them on a regular basis. In the end a challenge may have only a few well articulated and focused ideas associated with it, but one of which may be "the big one." I submit that a culture that encourages open discussion and ideation is more likely to land on "the big one" than a culture that does not encourage individuals to become "ideators."

Developing more ideas isn't something that just happens in a brainstorm session (in fact, there is a lot of evidence to suggest brainstorms are rarely where the best ideas originate). More important is a team attitude toward openness and collaborative thinking that permeates day-to-day interactions. Team members and the Zero-Gravity Thinker need to feel safe sharing their half-baked ideas with one another. And, critically, they need to be open to what Michelle Barton of the University of Michigan calls the "generous contribution." That is, they must be willing to offer ideas unselfishly, with the understanding that those ideas will be twisted, turned, morphed, changed, and (hopefully) improved by the group. In this way idea "ownership" shifts from the individual to the collective.

Consider what happens at MIT's Media Lab, where Professor Pattie Maes's team developed Firefly, a commercial system for filtering the products and music that users can find online based on the preferences of like-minded people. She says, "Most of the work we do is like this. We start with a half-baked idea which most people—especially critical people—would just shoot down right away or find uninteresting. But when we start working on it and start building, the ideas evolve."[2]

Unless, of course, we work in a culture where this type of openness is already accepted, sharing half-baked ideas can be easier said than done. The sad reality is that many of us, particularly more senior managers, have become so used to being "sold" on ideas that we actually participate very little in the ideation process itself—which can be a negative for everyone involved.

I used to work with a fellow named Jim, who was Ivy League educated and a very bright businessperson. Though I was initially unaware of it, Jim used to get very frustrated and confused by my occasional visits to his office, where I would bounce some new idea off of him. My modus operandi would be to ask, "What do you think of this . . . ?" and then proceed into a passionate outline of my latest brainstorm. For me this was just a way to clarify my thoughts and generate some discussion. Passionate as I might appear at the time, my objective in those discussions wasn't to "sell" him on a concept, but to enlist his brainpower in helping me think it through. He, on the other hand, thought I was trying to sell him. And when I would come in the next day with an idea that seemed to be the complete opposite of what we had just discussed, he began to question my judgment (if not my sanity).

Finally one day he stopped me and asked point blank if I was trying to convince him of a particular argument.

"No," was my surprised response, "I just want to get your thoughts on this."

Both of us had an epiphany then. I realized that Jim was used to people "pitching" ideas to him—not enlisting him in the ideation itself. I, on the other hand, needed to "talk through" ideas as a way to clarify and improve (and often disprove) them. What we agreed to that day was that I would preface my discussions with him by letting him know whether I wanted to get his buy-in or whether I just wanted to borrow his creative thinking capabilities. That discussion marked the beginning of a great collaborative relationship that allowed us to build on one another's ideas with great fluency.

Learn to embrace the half-baked idea.

The man with a new idea is a crank until the idea succeeds. — *Mark Twain*

Question 9: Incubation seems to be a frivolous stage. Why is it important?

Answer: If any stage is going to be left out, this is likely to be the one. But evidence suggests we shouldn't be so quick to discard it. The Roffey Park Management Institute in the UK says that most insights and ideas occur away from the office—where individuals are "dreaming and drifting and thinking about something else other than work."[3]

Incubation is important because we don't always process information that can lead to insights in a timely fashion (like during the middle of a critical meeting or brainstorming session). Perhaps this is because, as French mathematician Jules-Henri Poincaré believed, the combination of thoughts and ideas that lead to innovation happens largely at a subconscious level. To illustrate, Poincaré once relayed the story of his struggle to solve a mathematical problem. Frustrated, he eventually gave up and went to spend some time at the beach. Shortly after, while walking along the bluffs of the coast and thinking of something entirely unrelated, the solution came to him as if out of nowhere.[4] His belief and the consensus of many today is that even though the conscious mind may take a break from a riddle, the subconscious will still be very active in trying to solve it.

For those who want a more contemporary example, look to Bill Gates. Gates gives himself (or endures—depending on how you look at it) incubation time called Think Weeks twice a year. During these week-long periods he locks himself away—in near-isolation—in a Pacific Northwest cabin to review dozens of papers and ponder the state of technology. The results of his introspection have been no less than revolutionary, sparking Microsoft to develop its Internet browser, create a tablet PC, and start an online videogame business.[5]

For long projects, building several weeks of incubation time into the schedule is often extremely valuable. Brighthouse, for instance, devotes four of the sixteen weeks it spends on most projects to this task—time in which they simply "play" with ideas and bounce new concepts around as the mood strikes them. Some, as evidenced by the quote below from Leonardo da Vinci, would advocate a complete break from thinking about the challenge at all during incubation. But, whether you take a long or short break (telling the entire team to take an individual walk, for instance), whether you choose to consciously think about the challenge during that time frame, or whether you simply let it percolate in the subconscious while you do something else, don't discard the activity. In a world of increasingly sophisticated computing and communications technology, it is easy to forget that the human brain does not always provide the best or fastest solution when it is "always on."

> Every now and then go away, have a little relaxation, for when you come back to your work your judgment will be surer. Go some distance away because then the work appears smaller and more of it can be taken in at a glance and a lack of harmony and proportion is more readily seen.
> — *Leonardo da Vinci*

Question 10: What's the "Make It Real" stage?

Answer: The last stage of the process is to develop a plan that will turn idea-vapor into solid reality. The Make It Real stage doesn't mean that the idea has to be finally implemented. But it does mean that three things have to be firmly in place. First, a clear outline of the steps required to get from idea to implementation needs to be established. These steps can include everything from developing a prototype to securing funding or management support. Second, due dates and owners need to be assigned to each of the steps. Everyone on the team needs to understand who is accountable for what and when. Finally, there needs to be one overall owner for assuring that the project moves forward. Call them a champion, an advocate, or a sponsor, it doesn't matter. This is a senior person on the team who will help clear any management, resource, or other obstacles as well as act as overall project guardian—assuring that timetables are met and action keeps moving forward.

Question 11: Why might a Zero-Gravity Thinker in a Collaborate role fail?

Answer: Here are five of the primary reasons:

1. A team doesn't understand and/or accept the role and doesn't work collaboratively and open-mindedly with the outsider.
2. The leader doesn't show support for the Zero-Gravity Thinker or the type of different thinking and actions that result from the engagement.
3. The team and Zero-Gravity Thinker can't speak a common language fairly early in the process (i.e., when expertise isn't related enough).
4. Deliverable expectations are inappropriate for time, resources, or the Collaborate role.
5. Individual recognition is perceived as more important than team recognition. On that note, take a look at what one scientific laboratory is doing to stimulate collaboration:

> **Rewarding the Team**

In an effort to place more emphasis on collaborative work rather than on individual efforts, the Oak Ridge National Laboratory gives every author of a joint publication the same performance credit as those who write single author papers.[6] ∎

• KEY POINTS •

1. Set the Zero-Gravity Thinker up for success by assuring that the team has bought into the concept from the beginning. Remember that the effort must be collaborative or it will fail.

2. There are many processes that work well for stimulating innovative thinking depending on the challenge, the team, etc. Teams should look for a process that, at minimum, includes some element of the following steps:

> A focus on problem definition
> Immersion of the Zero-Gravity Thinker into the team and the challenge
> A solution-generation/ideation time frame
> Time for incubation
> A plan for turning the idea into reality

3. Leaders must stay closely aligned with and visibly supportive of the Zero-Gravity Thinker and the overall collaborative effort to improve the odds of a successful engagement.

CHAPTER 10

DO-IT-YOURSELF WEIGHTLESS THINKING

LOSING THE WEIGHT OF EXPERTISE ON YOUR OWN

The first and greatest victory is to conquer yourself;
to be conquered by yourself is of all things most
shameful and vile. — *Plato*

EVEN IF A TEAM ASKS a Zero-Gravity Thinker to play the Collaborate role for all of its Big P and Exploratory problems as well as for its most important and complex Little P problems, that amounts to only a handful (albeit a very important handful) of challenges. Sure, a bit of Zero-Gravity Thinker input here and there via the Teach, Facilitate, Inform, and Do roles can give a nice additional innovation boost, but the fact remains that most teams will face the majority of efforts on their own. In recognition of that fact, this chapter introduces six do-it-yourself (DIY) practices for thinking weightlessly. Teams whose members establish these practices as habits (with or without a Zero-Gravity Thinker involved) are very likely to strengthen their IQs (Innovation Quotients).

PRACTICE ONE: LOOK AT A CHALLENGE
· AS IF YOU ARE SOMEONE ELSE . . . ·
AND THEN SOMEONE ELSE . . .
AND THEN SOMEONE ELSE

A waiter, a fitness instructor, and a lawyer see a woman slip in a puddle of water in a busy restaurant. The woman is unhurt and the restaurant owner assumes he simply needs to be faster to mop up spills on the floor. But when each of the three witnesses is asked what problem the restaurant needs to address, they all give a very different response.

Waiter: The problem is that the restaurant needs to hire more wait-
staff so spills resulting from rushed service can be avoided.
Fitness Instructor: The problem is that the restaurant needs to
replace its slippery floors with floors that provide more trac-
tion.
Lawyer: The problem is that the restaurant needs to limit its liabil-
ity the next time this happens by posting signs telling patrons
to watch their step.

Whether any of these perspectives is better than the owner's is up to him. But without exposure to them, he can't even make the call. Obviously this is an example of the benefit of interacting with people who have different mindsets. But people can train themselves to adopt different mindsets, at least to an extent. In this story, although the owner's first response was to be faster with a mop, it's likely that if he were asked to "think like a lawyer," he would have come up with something similar to what the lawyer in this story suggested.

A favorite person that Yale professors Barry Nalebuff and Ian Ayres like to pretend to be is "Croesus" (rhymes with Jesus), who was king of Lydia (modern-day Turkey) from 560 to 556 B.C. Croesus was so wealthy that money would have been no obstacle for him in problem solving. By pretending to be this particular "someone else," Nalebuff and Ayres can explore ideas as if money were irrel-evant—a sometimes helpful way to become "weightless."[1]

Looking at this idea from a slightly different angle, forcing teams to be someone else is almost literally what Edward de Bono's "Six Thinking Hats" process does. The method, which has been used by organizations all over the world, is employed during team think-sessions. During the meetings, the entire team is asked to "wear" (this doesn't have to be literal though it can be) one color hat at a time. When the team is wearing a particular hat they are allowed to make comments only appropriate to the "perspec-tive" of that hat as outlined below:

White Hat: Neutral and objective, concerned with facts and figures
Red Hat: The emotional view based on gut feelings
Black Hat: Careful and cautious, the devil's advocate hat
Yellow Hat: Sunny and positive
Green Hat: Associated with fertile growth and new ideas
Blue hat: Cool, above everything else—the organizing hat[2]

De Bono asserts that "the main difficulty of thinking is confu-sion."[3] By encouraging thinkers to limit their view to one perspec-tive at a time, their thoughts and ideas can become more crystallized. Just as important, this process allows—even forces—participants to step outside their own mindset to "play" the role each hat represents. It's not precisely the same as pretending to be a lawyer or fitness instructor or waiter, but it does help people get outside of themselves.

Have your team slip on someone else's shoes for a while. They may be able to tap into Zero-Gravity Thinker capabilities they didn't even know they had.

PRACTICE TWO: TRAIN YOURSELF TO LOOK FOR WEIRD COMBINATIONS

The human brain cannot deliberately concentrate
on two separate objects or ideas without forming

a connection between them.[4] — *Michael Michalko,*
author of Thinkertoys

As discussed extensively, mentally juxtaposing seemingly unrelated patterns, objects, or concepts to generate new ideas is a powerful innovation tool. One of the most impressive recent examples of this power is the case of Burt Rutan and the development of Space-ShipOne (Figure 10-1). As many of you may recall, Rutan was CEO of Scaled Composites, the company that won the $10 million X-prize in 2005 for designing the first nongovernment vehicle to take a man into space.

One of the problems Rutan faced during the development of SpaceShipOne was figuring out how to get it to glide back to earth, nose down, after it had entered space. Rutan had been thinking about the problem for a while with no solution. Then one night when he was getting ready for bed, the thought of a badminton shuttlecock (I used to just call them birdies) popped into his head.

If you want to try a little experiment, throw one of those things up in the air. They always land nose down. That thought was what excited Rutan. He realized that if he designed SpaceShipOne with the same principles as a shuttlecock, he would have a way to assure a smooth landing for the space craft.[6] Admittedly, this wasn't a case of purposefully trying to juxtapose seemingly unrelated concepts together, and furthermore, it may very well have simply been the product of Rutan's brain incubating on the chal-

Figure 10-1. SpaceShipOne. "They said if NASA couldn't do it, then it couldn't be done" (X-prize judge Dezso Molnar).[5]

lenge subconsciously. But either way, Rutan made the most of it. He lingered on the juxtaposition long enough to recognize it as a solution to his problem—a solution worth $10 million and a place in history.

> Confidence in nonsense is a requirement for creativity since before a breakthrough is recognized most think it is nonsense.[7] — *Burt Rutan*

Or consider the case of Bette Nesmith. In 1951 Bette (who also happens to be the mother of Mike Nesmith of the musical group, The Monkees) invented liquid paper. How? By combining two very different concepts to solve a problem. At the time Nesmith was a secretary by day and an amateur artist by night. One day while typing a document at work she imagined how nice it would be if she could paint over her typing mistakes as easily as she painted over brush mistakes in her artwork. Based on that thought Nesmith put some paint in a nail polish bottle and brought it to work. Voila! An innovation that Gillette bought a few years later for $48 million dollars was born.[8]

Here's one last example. I was once managing a product line and was desperately trying to think of ways to stretch the limited advertising budget. One afternoon our finance director mentioned that we had excess inventory in one of our older product models that we were going to have to write off at considerable expense. Deciding to put to work the "weird juxtaposition" exercise I had recently learned, I started thinking about both problems at once: the need for more advertising and the negatives associated with excess inventory. In some ways, these seem like cause and effect aspects of the same problem! Too little advertising = too much unsold inventory.

However, what came to me as I considered the two challenges was that perhaps we could better address both problems if they were combined. So this is what we did. We struck a deal with one

▶The Unexpected in the Arts

The East Village Opera Company in New York fuses full-length opera performed in its original language with rock arrangements to produce a musical hybrid that has fans of both genres applauding. As I watched their grandiose performance one evening, I couldn't decide whether I was enjoying opera, a rock concert, or some version of musical theater. It didn't matter. The effect was such a fresh feast for my senses that I stopped trying to categorize it halfway through the first song—and just enjoyed. ■

of our major customers to take our excess inventory in exchange for running a certain amount of advertising for the product. Without getting into all of the accounting details, it ended up being a far better deal for us to get the advertising and the support of a major client than to simply write off the excess inventory. Chances are however, that I would never have thought of this idea if I hadn't purposefully tried to connect two seemingly disparate problems.

So, here's a concrete assignment. Practice thinking of a challenge and something as unrelated to the challenge as a tube of toothpaste, a hammer, or the sitcom you watched last night—simultaneously for at least five minutes every day. Let your mind wander. What does the seemingly unrelated item remind you of

➤ Weird Combos at P&G

Procter & Gamble is benefiting from proactively looking for ways to combine previously unrelated ideas. In their case, they search for ways to use technologies originally designed to solve one type of problem to solve totally unrelated problems in unrelated industries. They have used the electro-static technology used to paint cars, for example, to improve the way cosmetics can be applied to skin. And, Tide customers get every last drop out of their detergent bottles because P&G uses plasma technology—originally developed to repel dirt from plastic bumpers— for the inside of the containers.[9] ■

that might be valuable to your challenge? Whether practicing this alone or in a group (this can be a fun, funny, and sometimes surprisingly productive exercise to throw into a working session), it's almost guaranteed that you will feel silly initially. But I encourage you to be bold and stick with it. Most of the time nothing productive will come of the five minutes. The value, however, is in the habit. Over time it's likely you will train your mind to start connecting things in bizarre ways even when you're not trying to (in some ways this is like forcing yourself to have the low latent inhibition, referred to in Chapter 5, that is so often associated with highly creative people). That capability might lead to the breakthrough you're looking for. Or, it might just lead you to a more open mind. Either way, you're building up ExpertThink resistance!

To read about someone who spent a little more than just five minutes at a time trying to find connections between seemingly disparate fields, meet Greg Roger:

In 2004 Greg Roger was awarded the Australian Academy of Technological Sciences and Engineering (ATSE) Clunies Ross Award. The award honors innovators who have made significant contributions to Australian economics, environment, or society. Rogers' contributions sprang from his proactive decision to combine the disciplines of engineering and medicine.

Early in his career Rogers planned on becoming an orthopedic surgeon. During his time as an intern, however, he observed that surgeons had tremendous difficulty chiseling cement from old hip replacements. Rogers contemplated the problem with some engineering colleagues and developed a tool that cut the procedure time from hours to minutes.

Based on the success of that effort, Rogers reasoned that by purposefully combining key learnings from engineering with key learnings from medicine, he might uncover other innovative opportunities. Being something of an overachiever, Rogers decided to go all-out in enhancing his ability to combine ideas from these two realms. His approach was to combine his medical training with a masters degree in engineering.

Rogers' intuition proved right. He has been able to combine these two relatively disparate fields to develop over twenty patents and establish a $10 million business. More impressive is that his innovative thinking has improved the medical treatment of countless patients undergoing reconstructive surgery, heart valve insertion, hip replacement, and more.[10]

PRACTICE THREE: CHANGE THE WAY YOU THINK ABOUT THINKING

A senior Comcast executive once told me that he spends at least fifteen minutes every day just thinking. In fact, he said he relished airplane time because it gave him the opportunity to mull things over—a luxury it was hard to get in the office. Many of us have experienced this. In fact, some colleagues recently shared that they were dreading the fact that in-air e-mail is likely to become a standard capability in the not-too-distant future. So much for re-flection time.

One of the great misconceptions the workplace seems to foster is that visible action equals productivity; therefore, lack of visible action must mean nothing is happening. While this might be true for jobs in manual labor, which until the mid-to-latter part of the twentieth century most of us were engaged in, this is most cer-tainly not true for many occupations today.

The Dilbert comic strip shown below (Figure 10-2) is funny be-cause so many of us can relate to it. Who hasn't felt a little sheep-ish and even slightly guilty for being caught staring into space at the office? After all, when we think, there is no proof that we are actually working. But we are moving further and further into a new era, one in which the brute force of our actions has far less impact than the clever twists of our imaginations. Just as our speed, strength, and physical skills might have differentiated us as work-ers in the past, increasingly it is our ability to think, to connect ideas in new and imaginative ways, and to innovate that will set us apart. Yet we cling to the old paradigm.

In a June 2005 survey conducted by *CMO* (Chief Marketing Offi-cer) Magazine, the single greatest barrier senior marketing execu-tives cited as hindering their performance was lack of time for strategic thinking and planning.[11] A 2003 research study by *CIO*

Figure 10-2. Dilbert.

© Scott Adams/Dist. by United Feature Syndicate, Inc.

(Chief Information Officer) Magazine revealed that inadequate budgets and "lack of time for strategic thinking" were the biggest hurdles these executives faced in their technology roles for organizations.[12] And a blog posted by George Binney on the European Business Forum conveys the following story:

> With middle managers from a well-known multinational, I was watching a corporate video made by the chief executive. "Accelerate," he said, "we must go faster. The strategy has not changed. The goals are clear. We need to be bolder in the way we execute strategy if we are to get ahead of our competitors."
>
> Yet when I look around me at the managers in these companies . . . it doesn't seem to be lack of speed that is the problem. All of them are coping with tumultuous change—in their businesses, their organizations and their people. They all work long hours. On a recent development program, some worked till the early hours on their e-mails. Many said they were not happy with their "work/life" balance.
>
> One woman manager, for me, put her finger on it when she said, "We are moving so fast, when do we ever have time to think?" When indeed? When do managers get time to reflect, to think together on what is working, on what is not, and what needs to be done differently?[13]

Each of these examples highlights the fact that we know there is a significant problem. We just don't seem to know how to address it.

I don't have a magic solution. Like everyone else, I do the best I can to juggle multiple responsibilities and deadlines—starting with the things I consider most important. This leads to a practical suggestion. Make thinking time a priority. Nurture a culture that encourages—no, demands—that team members devote fifteen minutes a day to pondering a challenge, like the Comcast executive above. This doesn't mean writing out a "to-do" list associated with it. It means considering the bigger picture. It means considering the "what ifs" of potential solutions. It may even mean trying to make weird connections in your mind that will stimulate new insights.

Treat the fifteen minutes of daily "thinking time" like a high priority meeting. Schedule it on the calendar. Give employees signs to hang on their office or cubicle doors that say, "Please do not disturb. Thinking in progress." This isn't so far-fetched, by the way. A few years ago, Asda, a UK supermarket now owned by Wal-Mart, gave people signs to hang on their doors that said "Quiet please. I'm having an idea."[14] Or, here's another thought: A friend of mine pointed out that her best thinking time is when she's running. Her suggestion was that companies might get the benefit of a healthier workforce along with better thinkers if they just encouraged their employees to exercise more!

Regardless of how your team establishes its thinking time, if you are its leader, make it a habit to ask what weird ideas or potential solutions people came up with during this time. Don't ask for or expect anything meaningful out of most of the answers to that question. Instead, praise the bizarre reflection, the out-of-the-ordinary thought-tangent, the funky idea. Results are not likely to come predictably—and when they do come, they may not seem to be at all related to the "thinking" activity.

But by encouraging these practices, the team develops a culture that values the power of thought. Thinking time becomes a bonafide, high-priority activity. And though it may seem like the first thing that should go when there are 200 e-mails in the in-box and a crucial project due by the end of the week, that may be precisely the time when it is most important.

PRACTICE FOUR: SPEND QUALITY TIME
• DEFINING THE PROBLEM BEFORE •
TRYING TO SOLVE IT

We touched on this topic in Chapter 9 during the discussion of the problem-solving process. But, it is so important, it is worth revisiting in more detail here. As Michael Michalko, author of the cre-

►Thinking Companies

3M is famous for its 15 percent rule, the rule that encourages employees to spend 15 percent of their time at work thinking about and pursuing new ideas. Geoffrey Nicholson, 3M staff vice president of corporate technical planning and international technical operations, says "Some people don't use that time; some people take more. But it's not the 15 percent that's important. It's the message that it's OK to dream."[15]

Other companies are jumping on and benefiting from that "OK to dream" bandwagon. Google, for instance, encourages its employees to spend 20 percent of their time on projects that are personally interesting to them, but not directly tied to their jobs. Just one of the many benefits of the policy so far? Gmail, Google's innovative and highly successful new e-mail service. Somebody thought it up when they weren't doing their job. ■

ative thinking book *Thinkertoys*, says, "The more time you devote to perfecting the wording of your challenge, the closer you will be to a solution."[16] Morgan D. Jones, a former CIA analyst and author of *The Thinker's Toolkit,* agrees and relays the following story:

> A young man awoke one morning to find a puddle of water in the middle of his king-sized water bed. To fix the puncture, he rolled the mattress outdoors and filled it with more water so he could locate the leak more easily. But the enormous mattress, bloated with water and impossible to control on his steeply inclined lawn, rolled downhill, smashing into a clump of thorny bushes that poked holes in the mattress's rubbery fabric. Disgusted, he disposed of the mattress and its frame and moved a standard bed into his room. The next morning he awoke to find a puddle of water in the middle of the new bed. The upstairs bathroom had a leaky drain."[17]

The point is that the way a problem is defined guides the way people think about it. Spending more time on problem definition can result in more productive thinking from the beginning. This is one of the reasons that Foster-Miller, a company named by *Inc.* Magazine as one of the most innovative in America in 2002, allocates time to broadly defining the problem it is trying to address before the start of any project. Its creations range from a robot that performs critical functions in nuclear facilities to a net that's used by police to trap fleeing criminals. When asked how they come up with so many different types of innovations, president and chief operating officer William Ribich says they begin each project with the question, "What are we really trying to do?" He goes on to say, "That means we must stand back and define the objective in the broadest terms. For example, instead of saying "We need a new syringe," it may be better to say, "We need a means for introducing a drug below the skin."[18] Better defining the problem actually focuses the mind on new opportunities for solving it.

As already noted, some excellent innovation and ideation firms have developed detailed processes for identifying the root cause problem to be solved or opportunity to be addressed. However, following are two simple exercises that can help a team better define a challenge on their own. The first is "How Many Ways Can You Say It?" The second is the "Big Bang Approach."

How Many Ways Can You Say It?

Sometimes the very words we use are innovation-stifling because they are grounded in "what we know" versus "what we can imagine." An events team I once worked with phrased their problem as, "How do we increase the number of attendees at our conference?" With that definition, the team could have explored a variety of different solutions: different marketing techniques, a new pricing structure for the event, new programming elements, etc. The fact, however, that the definition left so many angles open for exploration was a signal to the team that they needed to reframe it a bit.

As it turned out after much discussion and contemplation, the real challenge was stated as, "How do we become a more relevant conference to our target audience?" That definition guided the team's innovative thinking energy in a totally new and more rewarding direction. Later they were able to revisit the challenge of increasing attendance, which as a result of their efforts around relevance, they found easier to successfully resolve.

Individual and team work sessions, sessions in which the problem is stated and restated in numerous ways, can stimulate surprising insights. I have found it valuable to spend as much as a half hour restating the problem numerous ways in order to help uncover the "real" issue. Regardless of how your team decides to approach problem definition, keep in mind that sometimes this exercise can point to the need for more information. Sometimes it becomes clear as the problem is being defined, that key questions needed to be answered or critical pieces of information needed to be gathered before a firm definition can be completed.

The Big Bang Approach

Another exercise that can help define a problem is called the "Big Bang Approach." Figure 10-3 is a graphic that illustrates the process. Like the theoretical big bang that created the universe, this approach explodes the challenge in a myriad of different directions before giving it form. Essentially it has three steps:

1. Initially define the problem.
2. Think divergently about the problem by asking multiple questions (similar but certainly not limited to those shown in the graphic) that deconstruct or "explode" it.
3. Based on the outcome of that exploration, converge on a crisply defined (and improved) definition of the problem.

As an example, consider the situation Einstein was presented with in Question 6 of Chapter 9. We can loosely define the problem he faced as "How do we stop the comet from destroying Earth?" Then we explode/deconstruct the problem by asking questions that help us put it in context. Take a look at the simplistic brainstorm

Figure 10-3. The Big Bang approach to problem definition.

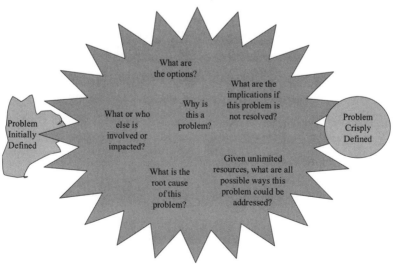

in Figure 10-4, based on some of the questions from the graphic. Please indulge the fact that the brainstorm answers reflect an assumption that the challenge is being faced today rather than during the actual lifetime of Einstein.

This simplistic example illustrates how a few questions about the nature of a problem can point to critical issues that need clarification—which can lead to a better problem statement, which might lead to more innovation solutions. A lot of the questions above didn't result in any particular insights for me (though they

Figure 10-4. Big Bang questions and brainstorm answers.

What or who else is involved or impacted?	Entire world - all governments, all people. Animal kingdom. Plant life, etc.
What are the options (who else could address this besides Einstein)?	Other scientists, military, NASA, other governments and space programs, private space programs
Why is this a problem?	Because entire Earth will be destroyed, or maybe (Einstein would need to get this clarified) because all life on Earth will be destroyed. Raises the question, is there a way for the comet to hit the Earth while life still survives?
What is the root cause of this problem?	Nature of comet paths. Nature of gravity. Impact may knock Earth out of orbit or cause it to explode. Impact may destroy nearby life and/or may create uninhabitable conditions on Earth.
What are the implications if this problem is not resolved?	Destruction of Earth and/or destruction of human race as well as other life on Earth.
Given unlimited resources, what are all possible ways this problem could be addressed?	Depends on the exact problem...Is the danger that a) the Earth itself will be destroyed by the impact of the comet or b) life on Earth will be destroyed by the impact and aftermath of the comet's impact?

might have for other people). But, when the question "Why is it a problem if the comet hits?" was asked, I realized I needed to understand whether the comet would destroy the Earth itself as a result of the impact or whether it would destroy life on Earth primarily as a result of the collision's aftermath. You may think this is splitting hairs since we're all dead either way, but the distinction could be crucial when trying to come up with a solution.

To take this a bit further: If the Earth itself is likely to survive the impact, but life is not, then the problem can be restated to, "How do we stop the comet from destroying life on Earth?" If the Earth is not likely to survive the impact, then the question might be phrased as, "How do we keep the comet from hitting Earth?" or "How do we keep the comet from hitting Earth with enough force to destroy it?" The point is that all of these different problem definitions would likely result in very different solution discussions. This approach is one way to help us hone in on the one definition that deserves our primary attention (Figure 10-5).

(*Note:* If this sounds like a movie, you've probably seen *Deep Impact*[19] or one of the other asteroid-hits-Earth flicks from the past decade or so. In *Deep Impact,* scientists tried to deflect asteroids that were on a collision course with Earth by using missiles.

Figure 10-5. The Big Bang approach: Asteroid example.

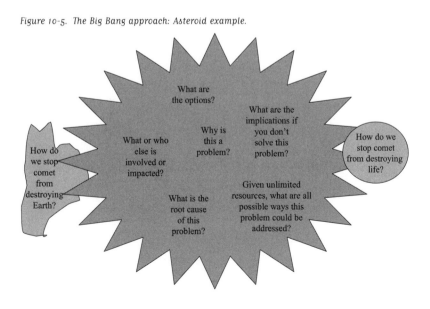

They also evacuated people, plants, and animals to underground caves as a way to salvage some life on Earth.)

PRACTICE FIVE: UNDERSTAND WHAT CONSTRAINS YOUR THINKING

The premise of this book is that we all get stuck in mindsets that constrain our thinking. A critical step, therefore, in being able to free ourselves is to identify the boundaries of our self-made prison. One tool that can help is the Assumptions and Constraints Box. It helps teams identify what's boxing them in.

Part 1. The Assumptions and Constraints Box

The Assumptions and Constraints Box (Figure 10-6) assumes that there are four categories of assumptions that constrain our thinking. Sometimes the constraints turn out to be real. Other times (surprise, surprise) they don't. The first two are what I call "laws"

Figure 10-6. The Assumptions and Constraints Box.

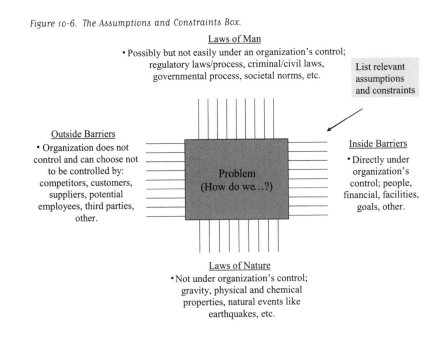

Laws of Man
• Possibly but not easily under an organization's control; regulatory laws/process, criminal/civil laws, governmental process, societal norms, etc.

List relevant assumptions and constraints

Outside Barriers
• Organization does not control and can choose not to be controlled by: competitors, customers, suppliers, potential employees, third parties, other.

Problem
(How do we...?)

Inside Barriers
• Directly under organization's control; people, financial, facilities, goals, other.

Laws of Nature
• Not under organization's control; gravity, physical and chemical properties, natural events like earthquakes, etc.

because they aren't under the immediate control of the organization and they can't be ignored.

➤*Laws of Nature* put natural limitations on us. For the most part, our organizations don't have control over them, but they certainly have an impact on (and can sometimes control) us. Think of a hurricane, a tsunami or, yes, even gravity (the natural kind, not the kind organizations make themselves!).

➤*Laws of Man* put man-made restrictions on us. Again, organizations don't control them (though they can certainly try to influence them), but these laws can have a major impact on the way a company does business. Think of tax laws, labor laws, regulations regarding communications, etc.

The other two categories are what I call "barriers." They do not control us and we can choose to ignore or sometimes change them, but they do impact our efforts.

➤*Outside barriers* are actions and circumstances within our business ecosystem. Actions like price cuts by competitors or price increases by suppliers are barriers that impact the way we think about and solve problems. A competitor's distribution strategy that outlines the type of retailer to whom they sell can be an outside barrier. Even the way customers perceive our product or service can be a barrier that puts constraints on our thinking.

➤*Inside barriers* are often the strongest barriers of all (given the content of this book, that probably won't surprise you). An organization's strategy and culture can have a marked impact on the types of solutions teams look for when problem solving. Politics, BKMs, and even relationships constrain us. The resources we've been allocated constrain us. Even such mundane things as planning cycles that tell us when it is OK to think strategically versus tactically can present barriers when we are problem solving.

The idea behind the Assumptions and Constraints Box is to get those laws and barriers out in the open where they can be examined and, yes, challenged—because sometimes what we think is firm and fixed turns out to be soft and pliable.

I have used this tool independently as well as in group discussions. Either way, Part 1 of this exercise is to get all of the assumptions and constraints on the table. Some teams will find some sides of the box more meaningful than others. "Laws of Nature" may not seem to affect a restaurant management team as much as an engineering team, for instance. I urge you, however, to spend time on all four sides. Understanding the mindset that drives your thoughts is the first step toward changing it. And sometimes constraints emerge that are quite surprising—constraints that are so much a part of the fabric of a culture that they are normally just perceived as background noise.

After all of the constraints are identified, move on to Part 2 of the exercise; the Reverse Constraints Exercise.

Part 2. The Reverse Constraints Exercise

This exercise forces us to think about the world as if the constraints we have categorized are turned upside down and inside out. Here's an example: Let's say that you are a human resources manager and you are trying to solve the problem of retaining more senior women in your workforce. You spend some time developing your Constraints and Assumptions Box. Figure 10-7 shows some examples a team might put in each category, though a completed box would be a lot fuller than this.

The Reverse Constraints Exercise starts with one of the constraints highlighted. For sake of illustration, I'll focus on a Laws of Nature constraint listed as:

> Women have babies and often want to spend time with their children after they are born.

The idea behind the exercise is to reverse each constraint statement captured in order to force the team to view it from a different perspective. In this case, I decided to state the reverse of the statement as:

Figure 10-7. The Assumptions and Constraints Box: Retaining senior women example.

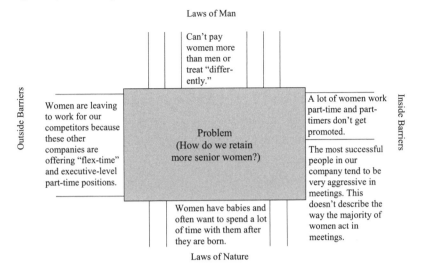

Men have babies and often want to spend time with their children after they are born.

With this statement in mind, I tried to imagine a pregnant Andy Grove or Bill Gates (pretty funny, huh?). Then I asked myself what Intel or Microsoft would have done to keep these men employed and productive if they were the ones who had babies. You can see just a few of the ideas I came up with in Figure 10-8.

Figure 10-8. Reverse constraints exercise.

Constraint or Assumption	Reverse Constraint or Assumption	Idea
Women have babies and want to be with their children.	Men have babies and want to be with their children.	Babies allowed in office; on-site nanny; daycare on every floor; family-lunches encouraged; liberal work-from-home policies; part-timers promoted at same rate as full-timers.

I'm not advocating any particular HR policy. In fact, I could have chosen a reverse statement—"Women have babies and don't want to spend time with their children"—which would have given me a completely different set of ideas to think about. But I am suggesting that this exercise is often eye-opening in terms of finding alternative solutions. Understanding what constrains our thinking and then forcing ourselves to imagine a world without that constraint is a powerful way to fight the gravity of "what we know."

> ►**HR Innovation: Babies in the Boardroom?**
>
> Although babies in the boardroom might not be very practical, it's really not so far-fetched. The UNCLE credit union (whose name derives from the University of California Lawrence Livermore Laboratory) in Pleasanton, California instituted a "Babies in the Workplace" policy in 2003, which allows parents to bring their babies to work with them until the child is eight months old or crawling (whichever comes first). The policy is credited with reducing the need for temporary workers and has also helped employees reduce childcare expenses. Based largely on this policy, the local Chamber of Commerce honored the company with its 2003 Family Friendly Employer of the Year award.[20] ∎

PRACTICE SIX: NURTURE THE ZERO-GRAVITY THINKER WITHIN

Two habits to practice:

1. *Broaden yourself.* Try to cultivate your own renaissance tendencies. Become an avid reader of both fiction and nonfiction. Pick up a magazine or explore a website that you normally wouldn't find interesting. Find a subject that intrigues you outside of work and really research it. Become an avid traveler. Visit foreign countries. Study another language. Take a day-trip to a part of your home state you've never visited before. Subscribe to a travel magazine or just read about a country you've never visited. By broadening yourself you enhance the chances that you will be able to combine ideas in a way that will significantly impact the future.

2. *Discipline yourself to react with two positives for every one negative response to an idea.* This is tough. It's much easier for us to poke holes in new ideas than to figure out how they might work. So, challenge yourself and others on your team to adopt this 2-for-1 policy. This doesn't mean you have to think every idea is good. But it does mean you have to look for the good that might be in every idea—even if you do so for only a moment or two. The 2-for-1 habit helps make the "half-baked" idea-sharing discussed in Question 8 of Chapter 9 more effective. By forcing yourself to search for the kernel of insight that may not be well articulated in an initial idea statement, you are doing two things:

First, you are validating the contribution of the person who generated the idea. If each new concept is seriously contemplated, people will feel more open about sharing.

Second, you are exercising your thinking muscles. When your first reaction to an idea is negative, it usually means the idea doesn't mesh with your existing mindset. By forcing yourself to find something helpful in the concept, you are often stretching out of your comfort zone. And that is what weightless thinking is all about.

> Man cannot discover new oceans unless he has the courage to lose sight of the shore. — *André Gide, winner of the 1947 Nobel Prize for Literature*

• KEY POINTS •

This chapter highlights six practices teams can employ to help them escape the bounds of "what they know"—even without the help of a Zero-Gravity Thinker.

1. Pretend to view the problem as if you are someone else.
2. Practice making weird connections between ideas, objects, etc.
3. Learn to respect "thinking time."
4. Devote quality time to defining the problem before solving it.
5. Understand what constrains your thinking.
6. Nurture the Zero-Gravity Thinker within.

....

CHAPTER 11

THE COURAGE TO GO WHERE NO ONE HAS GONE BEFORE

THE ROLE OF THE LEADER

> If you continue to believe as you have always
> believed, you will continue to act as you have
> always acted. If you continue to act as you have
> always acted, you will continue to get what you
> have always gotten. If you want different results in
> your life or your work, all you have to do is change
> your mind. — *Anonymous*

BASEBALL FANS PROBABLY KNOW Billy Beane as the unorthodox general manager of the Oakland Athletics (more commonly known simply as the Oakland A's). But for students of innovation theory, Beane may be, at least in some respects, the model leader, hungry enough for a leg up on the competition to listen intently to and then implement any promising idea, even if it flies in the face of long-standing BKMs and time-tested wisdom.

For those who are unfamiliar with Beane, he was a baseball player who bounced back and forth between the majors and the minors during the 1980s before becoming part of the "administration" in the early 1990s. What makes Beane so special however, is not what he did as a player, but what he did as part of the administration. He turned one of the poorest teams in baseball (with a

2002 payroll of about $40 million versus the richest team's pay-roll—that of the New York Yankees—of about $126 million that same year) into one of the most successful teams. How? By ignoring conventional wisdom and listening to outsiders.

• HITTIN' OUT OF THE PARK •

The short version of the story is that Beane knew he couldn't compete for the best players available with teams who had three times his payroll budget. So perhaps with the mentality that he had nothing to lose, he began to disregard the expertise of baseball traditionalists in favor of what a new breed of baseball outsiders was promoting: a deeper, more sophisticated analysis of the game and its components than had ever been conducted before. Though the baseball establishment had been keeping "stats" for years, these outsiders saw the old data as woefully incomplete—able to tell only a partial story of what contributed to runs and outs. In fact, these renegades believed their new and improved way of looking at the game would result in fundamental changes in the way it was played and—most critically for the A's— staffed.

Beane became a convert. But it wasn't easy. Based on that conversion, he encountered incredulity among some of his own staff and derision among his counterparts on other major league teams. Nevertheless, under Beane's new vision, the A's started re-cruiting players who didn't fit the mold the traditional stats had cast. They didn't recruit players who looked a certain way. (Beane once joked with his scouts that they were trying to sell jeans rather than find the best players to draft.[1]) They didn't believe, as conven-tional baseball wisdom dictated, that college experience was a dis-advantage. And they paid far more attention to a player's past statistics than to the highly subjective but widely relied upon scouting assessment of "future potential." Based on a new way of looking at the world, the Oakland A's recruited players who were older, slower, and even pudgier than the competition. Of course, they were also cheaper, but this off-setting factor wasn't initially enough for Beane to be considered a great visionary.

As Michael Lewis says in his book, *Moneyball,* about one Oakland A's pick who didn't mesh with the established way of thinking during a league-wide teleconferenced drafting session, "If he [the A's scouting director, Erik Kubota] leaned in just a bit more closely [to the speaker phone] he might hear phones around the league clicking off, so that people could laugh without being heard. For they do laugh."[2]

Billy Beane has guts. And perhaps that is the most important attribute a leader brings to the table where innovation is concerned. Mel Perel, former director of innovation and commercialization at Ohio-based Batelle, a global science enterprise that develops and commercializes technology and manages laboratories for customers, said that a major impediment to sustained innovation in companies is lack of courage at the most senior levels. Courage, he suggests, "means shedding the complacency of traditional, comforting ways of thinking and doing. . . . It requires decisions and actions that actually accomplish something that few others are willing to try for fear of the consequences of failure."[3]

• MIXED MESSAGES •

Beane's decision to buck conventional baseball wisdom wasn't undertaken lightly. Though the evidence was highly compelling that traditional stats were, at best, inadequate, major league baseball had yet to be convinced. And so Beane surrounded himself with smart people who understood mathematical modeling and statistics. His "risk" was undertaken with foresight and planning. Yet, a risk it still was, as is the case with any innovation. In a recent study by innovation consultancy, Doblin, it was reported that only 4.5 percent of all innovation efforts met ROI goals established by the companies that funded them.[4] That means, of course, that over 95 percent of efforts failed. Not a great batting average, but to a large extent it is simply the nature of the game. So, good leaders have to be courageous and encourage their organizations to try new things. But they must at the same time be cognizant of the fact that a large percentage of their efforts will fail.

And this is where there tends to be a disconnection. Leaders want innovation, but they can be unwilling to accept that a huge amount of failure is an inevitable outcome of the effort. In an attempt to reduce risk, they cling to—and encourage their subordinates to cling to—what they know and are comfortable with. They even punish behavior that strays away from those norms if, as is statistically likely, it results in failure. According to innovation strategist, Clayton Christensen, "Managers who back ideas that flop often find their prospects for promotion effectively truncated. In fact, ambitious managers hesitate even to propose ideas that senior managers are not likely to approve. If they favor an idea that their superiors subsequently judge to be weak, their reputation for good judgment can be tarnished among the very executives they hope to impress."[5]

Obviously there is a problem. Leaders cannot give the order to innovate along with the unspoken, yet implicitly understood caveat

GREGORY

"I'd like your honest, unbiased and possibly career-ending opinion on something."

"without failing" and expect anything good to come from it. Not only is the order impossible to fulfill the vast majority of the time, but the silent "without failing" directive is itself an impediment to innovation. What it amounts to is an order to fail safely, i.e., since failure is likely anyway, set the effort up not to look too bad when things go sour. Plan to fail doing something the boss, the boss's boss, and the boss's boss's boss will agree with. Sounds like a real recipe for breakthroughs, doesn't it?

• A CULTURE OF COURAGE •

John Manferdelli, who was mentioned in Chapter 8 as the head of Microsoft's new business incubation efforts, recently told me that leaders "have to be willing to live with what, on a balance sheet, looks like failure." His philosophy is that even if ideas don't work out, they should be rewarded. New ideas, trials, and experimentation set the stage for an organization's future growth.

As a case in point, several years ago Intel entered the consumer products market with a barrage of offerings—from home networking kits to cameras to toys—none of which are still on the market today. Some would call Intel's innovation efforts in that space a colossal failure. But I would argue that in the long run Intel may gain more than it lost from that admittedly costly run of experiments. Why? For one thing, because technologies originally developed for use in stand-alone consumer products became high-value differentiating features in Intel's core chip products. The home networking technology, for instance, which had been sold in a retail kit to consumers, provided the communications foundation for Intel's breakthrough Centrino chipset—you know, the thing that lets your PC connect wirelessly to the Internet. This is relatively small potatoes, though compared to the other asset Intel gained, a modicum of wisdom. It is wisdom about consumers and technology that may prove to be pivotal as the company seeks to add increasing layers of value to its products in an effort to stave off the threat of commoditization.

Knowing that you don't know everything can be a powerful lesson. And, in some way, it may have been the disappointment of Intel's innovation efforts in the consumer products space that partially influenced the decision to appoint Paul Otellini, a sales and marketing veteran, to the CEO office. If that's the case, the ripple-effect-value of this particular "failed" innovation effort has yet to be seen.

From a leadership standpoint then, the answer is clear (though undoubtedly easier said than done). To foster innovation, leaders need to stop sending the message to innovate without failing. One way to do this is to visibly celebrate innovation efforts—whether they succeed or not. Software titan Intuit, for instance, regularly and boisterously bestows the "Greatest Failure Award" to employees who have spearheaded efforts that, to put it kindly, were less than successful, *but that the company learned from anyway.* This isn't to say that failure should be an objective, but making an outstanding effort and taking a risk should be. As Lou Lehr, 3M's CEO from 1978 to 1986, said: "As befits a company that was founded on a mistake, we have continued to accept mistakes as a normal part of running a business. Every single one of my colleagues in senior management has backed a few losers along the way. It's important to add, however, we expect our mistakes to have originality. We can afford almost any mistake once."[6] The point? When leaders ask their teams to innovate, they must leave off the "without failing" caveat. And let everyone know they mean it.

The other thing leaders can do is implement and become an avid proponent of recommendations like the ones in this book. Recognizing the handicap human nature has saddled us with when it comes to innovation isn't a weakness. It is empowering. It tells us when reinforcements are needed. It reminds us that our own expertise may blind us to new realities.

Success affects the way executives make decisions. It makes them overconfident, rigid in their beliefs, and reluctant to listen to people with differing views.[7] — *Pino G. Audia, University of California at Berkeley, Haas School of Business*

STAGED APPROACH TO INNOVATION-STIMULATION

For leaders who want to implement the concepts presented here, I suggest a staged approach that builds from the most basic innovation-stimulation tactics to advanced efforts involving Zero-Gravity Thinkers (Figure 11-2). As an organization progresses it should continue the actions of previous steps while adding new ones.

Basic (Ability to Defy Gravity: Poor)

First, establish the basics. This means doing what management and innovation strategists have been advising for years: Build teams of diverse people, encourage dissent and discussion, and actively seek out the contrary point of view. Sometimes, if your intuition tells you to, do the opposite of what culture and habit dictate—and give your teams leeway to do the same. If your organization is inclined to be persuaded by those who speak loudly and think quickly in meetings, make it a point to seek out the input of those

Figure 11-2. Staged approach to innovative thinking.

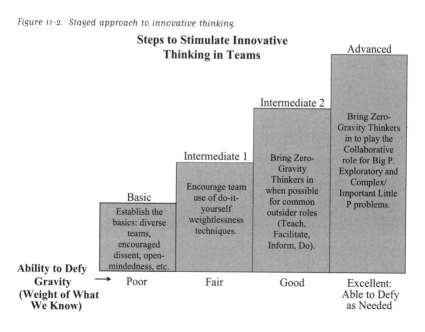

Steps to Stimulate Innovative
Thinking in Teams

who are quieter and prefer to respond after having more reflection time (where complex issues are concerned, the faster response is not necessarily the smarter one). If your group tends to listen more closely to those who are skilled presenters or to those who have the most powerful internal connections, look to the awkward speaker and less politically astute for advice. The only way to change mindsets is to change habits.

Most importantly, leaders must role-model an acceptance of and appreciation for new ideas. Cut the attitude that makes the half-baked idea unwelcome. As Professor Charlan Jeanne Nemeth of the University of California at Berkeley states, "There needs to be a 'welcoming' and not just a tolerating of dissent."[8]

What does that mean in terms of how a leader should behave? Take a look at the following story:

> David Perkins, a professor at Harvard's Project Zero, the center for the study of human cognitive potential, agreed to meet a young man to talk about a new idea. He wanted the young man to be comfortable, so the first thing he did was choose a casual, unintimidating restaurant in which to meet. He then listened to the idea very attentively. Afterwards, he sat quietly for a while and gave the idea some thought. Then he outlined all of the positive possibilities of the idea. Once he did that, he could then talk about some of his concerns (which were considerable), and the young man felt like these were just small issues to be resolved—not insurmountable obstacles that would discourage him from thinking further about the idea. David Perkins gave this young man inspiration to continue to think innovatively."[9]

To put the basics in place, start by making David Perkins your role model.

Intermediate 1 (Ability to Defy Gravity: Fair)

Once a leader has tackled the basics, things can be kicked up a notch by becoming active in sponsoring of the type of do-it-your-self (DIY) techniques presented in Chapter 10.

➤Reward team members who talk about the challenge as if they are Croesus or their grandmother or even a character from a movie they watched last week. Make this exercise part of team discussions.

➤Actively encourage team members to spend five minutes a day trying to draw connections between disparate objects or ideas. Spend five minutes of a staff meeting on this effort. Encourage and reward the silly and inane as well as the insightful

➤Encourage thinking time. Pass out signs that say "Please Do Not Disturb—Thinking in Progress." Then use them yourself every day in a visible manner. Make a point of publicly praising people whom you have seen use the signs. Good naturedly joke about the silly ideas you came up with while practicing the exercise. Respond appreciatively when someone shares their "insights" with you in kind. By adopting these practices you are creating a safe environment for sharing the kind of weightless thinking that over time can lead to innovations and insights.

➤Insist on a thoughtful approach to problem definition—especially for Big P and important/complex Little P challenges. Do not condone the "ready, fire, aim" tactics that are so popular. Ask team members how they defined the challenge, what steps they went through, etc. When reviewing a project timeline, insist that adequate problem definition time be scheduled. Hold the team accountable for examining the situation from all angles.

➤Make the team responsible for being able to articulate what constrains their thinking with regard to a specific challenge. Acknowledge and reward teams that walk through the Constraints and Assumptions exercise. Participate with them if possible to better understand your own hang-ups about the situation.

➤Strengthen your renaissance tendencies and reward those on your team who do likewise. Make it fun. Have everyone on the team put a piece of paper in a hat telling what they did during the last month to strengthen their ability to generate "creative intersections." Maybe it was "I read a book by Henry Miller" or "I visited a Planetarium"—doesn't matter what. Pick one of the names out of the hat, congratulate the person on their renaissance tendency-building effort and then give them a small gift, such as movie tickets, coffee coupons, or a small gift certificate. The idea is to recognize the importance of these "outside" and "fun" activities as essential to building the kind of passionate, curious, and creative people that will help an organization flourish.

Intermediate 2 (Ability to Defy Gravity: Good)

If you've implemented or are at least trying to implement the first two steps, it's time to think about Zero-Gravity Thinkers. Start by at least considering the three Zero-Gravity-Thinker characteristics (psychological distance, renaissance tendencies, and related expertise) any time you are filling the Teach, Facilitate, and Inform roles. Consider making these characteristics a priority when bringing in someone to Do what your team can't.

And when an outsider with these characteristics does join the team, make sure they understand that their ability to provide a unique point of view is part of what you value about them. This discussion is your opportunity to express your enthusiasm for and openness to any out-of the-ordinary ideas they might bring to the effort—with the understanding, of course, that their primary job is still to Teach, Facilitate, Inform, or Do.

By the way, a side effect of this discussion is that it is likely to boost the outsider's confidence in their creative capacity—which will actually enhance it. Someone else's expectations are powerful things, even for the most successful, mature, and jaded of us. In fact, leaders should take note that research conducted by numerous academics, including professors Pamela Tierney of Portland State University and Steven M. Farmer of Wichita State University, suggests that a supervisor's expectations with regard to the creative capability of her employees contributes significantly to their actual creative performance.[10]

Advanced (Ability to Defy Gravity: Excellent)

The last step is to start engaging Zero-Gravity Thinkers in the Collaborate role for Big P, complex/important Little P, and Exploratory problems. Here are a few high-level considerations.

First, commit to testing the concept over several projects. Track the process and learn from it as you go. Recognize that every effort, every team, and every Zero-Gravity Thinker will be different. Let the Zero-Gravity Thinker and team work out the best process and working relationship to meet each project's end-objectives based on their assessment of all the variables.

Second, be advised that the role of the leader is perhaps more crucial to the success of the collaborative Zero-Gravity-Thinker engagement than the Zero-Gravity Thinker himself. As already noted, in order for teams to feel comfortable questioning their basic beliefs and challenging the authority of experts inside and outside the company, leaders have to be role models of open-mindedness. In this regard, a leader's actions can be more powerful than words. Visible support for experimental processes and even dead-end idea explorations indicate a leader's understanding that trial and error are a necessary and even valuable part of the effort. And the leader's obvious support of the Zero-Gravity Thinker (through ongoing interaction with this person after he is on board) lends credibility to this outsider's inputs.

Third, just accept it. Leaders have a tough job, particularly where innovation is concerned. Not only must they be courageous in blazing new trails themselves, but they also need to be role models who will instill bravery in those around them.

• MAKING OUR OWN LUCK •

Serendipity is something we haven't discussed much in this book. But it is, of course, an undeniable factor in many breakthrough insights and innovations. An English author named Horace Walpole first used the term in a letter he wrote in 1754. He based the term on the title of a fairy tale, "The Three Princes of Serendip," a story of three princes who continuously make fortuitous, if unintended, discoveries as they travel. But smart leaders understand quite well the difference between fairy tales and reality. They know that to a large degree, as Louis Pasteur said, "chance favors only the prepared mind." By bringing in outsiders with specific characteristics at specific times to play specific roles for a team, leaders can be better prepared to fight the potentially innovation-lethal effects of, well, human nature. Unlike the princes of Serendip, most of us aren't the recipients of unplanned, continuous good fortune. Zero-Gravity Thinkers help us make our own luck.

Brilliance is not eternal. — *Larry Fox, Intel Corporation*

• KEY POINTS •

1. Leaders must sometimes be courageous enough to ignore convention, and act on their own intuition and on the rational arguments of outsiders in order to innovate.

2. Leaders can unintentionally thwart innovation in their teams by giving the order to innovate along with the unstated but implicitly understood caveat: *without failing.*

3. Leaders must stop giving this contradictory order (explicitly or implicitly) and model appropriate levels of risk-taking and experimentation in order to instill the courage to innovate in their teams.

RELATED EXPERTISE GRID

AS NOTED IN CHAPTER 6, there might not be a perfect formula for determining the exact type of related expertise a Zero-Gravity Thinker should have for any particular project. However, one framework I have found useful in some situations is the Related Expertise Grid.

The grid assumes that two variables are most important in considering the type of expertise likely to be relevant to a business challenge: functional expertise and industry expertise.

Functional expertise is expertise in such functional areas as marketing, manufacturing, strategic planning, finance, product development, and human resources. Users of the grid can get as granular as they think useful in defining functional expertise. For instance, instead of defining marketing as one function, market research might be one function, marketing communications another, and promotional marketing a third.

Industry expertise is expertise in the industry a challenge is most closely aligned with, such as semiconductors, banking, or health care. In using the grid, I have even defined the term much more broadly to mean the environment in which expertise has been applied. For instance, instead of listing "health care" as the industry, I might find it useful to list "doctor's office" or "pathology lab" or "emergency room" as the industry. I have also defined "industry" in a way that is far more segmented than is typical. For instance, instead of saying "consumer products industry," I might say "flashlight industry" (as I did in the Eveready Battery Company story in Chapter 6). "Industry," as used in this grid, therefore, is a broad term to mean the context in which experience has been applied. Users of the grid can experiment with the optimal definition for their particular situation.

The grid assumes that the functional and industry expertise most relevant to a challenge would be closest to the x/y intersection (Figure A-1). As expertise becomes less relevant to a challenge it falls farther out on the grid. Most teams are composed of people

Figure A-1. Related expertise grid.

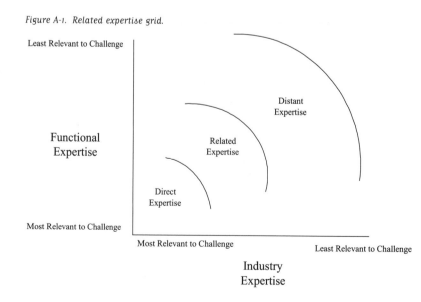

who fall into what the figure shows as "direct expertise." People who fall into the "distant expertise" area of the graph might have some difficulty "speaking the same language" as other team members. Those who fall in the "related expertise" zone are Zero-Gravity-Thinker candidates.

Leaders can use this grid as a way to think about the type of expertise that is most relevant to their challenge as well as what types of functional and industry expertise might be related. What can sometimes be interesting from a Zero-Gravity-Thinker standpoint is to look for direct expertise that is aligned on one dimension (functional or industry) and related expertise on the other dimension. And, keep in mind that people with "distant expertise" can sometimes provide stimulating input if a person with related expertise can bridge the communications gap between the distant expert and the team. In fact, some organizations, like the Global Innovation Network mentioned in Chapter 7, regularly act as translators between those with distant expertise and the client team—as a way to stimulate highly innovative thinking.

Let's look at a quick example. If, for instance, Henry Ford had graphed the expertise of Walter Flanders (see Chapter 6) using this tool, it might have looked something like Figure A-2. Ford might have ranked the relevancy of various functions and industries to the manufacturing challenges his team faced in a way similar to what is illustrated in this figure. He might then have been able to pinpoint where Flanders fit in this particular view. Flanders, as the figure shows, had direct expertise in manufacturing and related expertise in sewing machine industry—placing him firmly in the "related expertise" space.

Though this is a largely intuitive exercise, what can be enlightening, either prior to looking for a Zero-Gravity Thinker or when evaluating the "fit" of a particular candidate for the job, is the thought process it requires. In order to determine what expertise might be related, a leader must get a clear view of what is direct. This requires some reflection on the challenge. What is the true problem? What other industries or functions might offer valuable

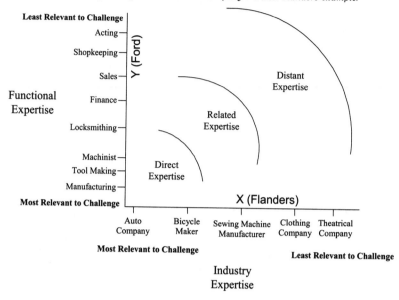

Figure A-2. Related expertise grid: Ford Motors Company / Walter Flanders example.

insights for solving it? If the problem is defined differently, how does the graph change in terms of how relevant specific industries or functions are to the challenge?

Again, though not a perfect tool, the grid can be helpful to those of us who benefit from a visual thinking guide.

A LEADER'S GUIDE

TO GET THE MOST OUT of a Zero-Gravity-Thinker collaborative engagement:

1. Start by carefully considering what you want from the effort. Make sure your expectations are reasonable based on the time frame and resources available.
2. Before recruiting a Zero-Gravity Thinker to play the Collaborate role, make sure the team understands the role and has bought in to the effort.
3. During the recruiting process for a Zero-Gravity Thinker, work with the candidate to agree on deliverables, time frames, and overall expectations. Make sure you both know how success will be measured. Involve the team in the hiring decision.

4. Set up regular (typically weekly) status meetings with the Zero-Gravity Thinker to see how things are progressing, provide insights, and refine goals and deliverables if necessary. Leaders who pawn the outsider off on subordinates and fail to interact with her may be setting the engagement up for failure.

5. Gather informal feedback from the team as the project progresses and provide this to the Zero-Gravity Thinker to help him improve processes, relationships, etc.

6. When the project is complete, have a post-mortem discussion with the Zero-Gravity Thinker, outlining what worked well and what could have been improved. This dialogue will be helpful not only for the outsider, but for the team as they assess their ability to benefit from this type of engagement in the future.

7. Finally, reward the work of the group, not of individuals. Even if a particular person seems to be responsible for the "big idea," that person was likely stimulated by interaction with other people on the team. Where innovation and a collaborative effort with a Zero-Gravity Thinker are concerned, each person shares in the success and failures of the whole.

NOTES

....

• INTRODUCTION •

1. William J. Baumol, "Education for Innovation: Entrepreneurial Breakthroughs vs. Corporate Incremental Improvements" (National Bureau of Economic Research, April 30, 2004). www.nber.org

2. Benjamin F. Jones, "The Burden of Knowledge and the Death of the 'Renaissance Man': Is Innovation Getting Harder?" (Northwestern University, October 19, 2004).

• CHAPTER 1 •

1. Bruce Nussbaum, "How to Build Innovative Companies," *BusinessWeek*, August 1, 2005.

2. *The McKinsey Quarterly*, "What Global Executives Think About Technology and Innovation," August 2005. www.lwcresearch .com/filesfordownloads/GlobalExecsThinkAboutInnovation.pdf

3. *Source*: Coca-Cola Company website: www.cocacola.com

4. Irving L. Janis, *Groupthink*. (Boston: Houghton-Mifflin Company, 1982).

5. Clayton Christensen, *The Innovator's Dilemma* (Boston: Harvard Business School Press, 1997).

6. Dorothy Leonard and Walter Swap, "When Sparks Fly: Igniting Creativity in Groups" (Boston: Harvard Business School Press, 1999).

• CHAPTER 2 •

1. Irving L. Janis, *Groupthink*. (Boston: Houghton-Mifflin Company, 1982).

2. Janis, *Groupthink*.

3. Ibid.

4. Excerpt from *A Thousand Days: John F. Kennedy in the White House* by Arthur M. Schlesinger, Jr. Copyright © 1965, and renewed 1993 by Arthur M. Schesinger, Jr. Reprinted by permission of Houghton-Mifflin Company. All rights reserved.

5. Permanent Subcommittee on Investigations of the Committee on Governmental Affairs, U.S. Senate, "The Role of the Board of Directors in Enron's Collapse," July 8, 2002.

6. From a July 7, 2002 press release by Carl Levin, chairman, and Susan M. Collins, ranking minority member of the Senate's Permanent Subcommittee on Investigations

7. James Surowiecki, "Board Stiffs," *The New Yorker*, March 8, 2004. www.newyorker.com / talk / content / articles / 040308ta_talk_ surowiecki

8. S. Asch, "Effects of Group Pressure upon the Modification and Distortion of Judgments," in *Groups, Leadership and Men: Research in Human Relations*, H. Guetzkow (Pittsburgh, Pa.: Carnegie Press, 1951).

9. From Stanford Prison Experiment website. www.prisonexp .org/ Reprinted with permission of Phil Zimbardo.

10. *Science* 306, 5701 (2004): 1482-1483.

11. Princeton University press release, November 25, 2004.

12. Reprinted with permission of Roger Boisjoly.

13. Ibid.

14. Kathy Sawyer and R. Jeffrey Smith, "NASA's Culture of Certainty," *Washington Post*, March 2, 2003. www.globalsecurity.org/ org/news/2003/030302-shuttle01.htm

15. Report of the Government's Columbia Accident Investigation Board, 2003.

16. Richards J. Heuer, Jr., "Psychology of Intelligence Analysis" (Central Intelligence Agency: Center for the Study of Intelligence, 1999). www.odci.gov/csi/books/19104/index.html

17. News release—Administrative Office of the U.S. Courts, November 14, 2003. www.uscourts.gov/Press_Releases/fy03bk.pdf.

18. Peter F. Drucker, *The Effective Executive* (New York: Harper & Row, 1967), p. 148.

• CHAPTER 3 •

1. *Fortune* 151, March 21, 2005, p.104.

2. Peter A. Joy and Kevin C. McMunigal, "Ethics," *Criminal Justice* Magazine 18, 1 (Spring 2003). © 2003 by the American Bar Association. www.abanet.org/crimjust/spring2003/ethics.html

3. C. Ronald Huff, "Wrongful Conviction. Causes and Public Policy Issues," *Criminal Justice* Magazine 18, 1 (Spring 2003). © 2003 by the American Bar Association. www.abanet.org/crimjust/spring 2003/conviction.html

4. Allan W. Snyder, "Breaking Mindset" (Centre for the Mind, 1996). www.centreforthemind.com/publications/Breaking_Mindset .cfm

5. Ibid.

6. Diane Vaughn, *The Challenger Launch Decision: Risky Tech-*

nology, *Culture and Deviance at NASA* (Chicago: University of Chicago Press, 1996).

7. F. Summerfield, "Paying the Troops to Buck the System," *Business Month,* May 1990, pp. 77-79.

8. Robert Cialdini, "The Perils of Being the Best and the Brightest," *Harvard Management Communication Newsletter,* May 1990.

9. Stanley Milgram, *Obedience to Authority* (New York: Harper & Row, 1974).

10. Leonard Karakowsky and Kenneth McBey, "Do My Contributions Matter: The Influence of Imputed Expertise on Member Involvement and Self-Evaluations in the Workgroup," SAGE Publications: *Group & Organization Management* 26, 1 (2001): 70-92.

11. Charlan Nemeth and Jack Goncalo, "Influence and Persuasion in Small Groups" (University of California at Berkeley: Institute of Industrial Relations Working Group Series, 2004).

12. W. Bernard Carlson, "Inventor of Dreams," *Scientific American,* March 2005, pp. 79-85.

13. "Corporate Fraud and Abuse Taxes," *Public Citizen's Congress Watch,* September 10, 2002.

14. Columbia Accident Investigation Board, August 2002.

15. 2003 Kimberly-Clark Annual Report.

16. Peter Burrows, "Oh, Do I Love My iMac: Is Steve Jobs' Hip Hit the Start of Something Big at Apple?" *BusinessWeek,* October 5, 1998.

17. Ibid.

18. Andrew Hargadon, *How Breakthroughs Happen: The Surprising Truth About How Companies Innovate* (Boston: Harvard Business School Press, 2003).

• CHAPTER 4 •

1. Anahad O'Connor, "Pressure to Go Along with Abuse Is Strong but Some Soldiers Find Strength to Refuse," *New York Times,* May 14, 2004.

2. Robert I. Sutton," Weird Ideas That Work: 11½ Practices for Promoting, Managing and Sustaining Innovation" (New York: Free Press, 2002).

3. Charlan Jeanne Nemeth, "Managing Innovation: When Less Is More" *California Management Review* 40, 1 (Fall 1997).

4. *Source*: Phyllis McGinley, 1905-1978.

5. From the Australian Academy of Technological Sciences and Engineering Clunies Ross Foundation. www.storiesofinnovation .org/

6. *Multi Housing News*, October 1, 2003. www.multi-housing news.com/multihousing/search/article_display.jsp?vnu_content_id = 1986288

7. Irving L. Janis, *Groupthink*. (Boston: Houghton-Mifflin Company, 1982).

8. Donald Pelz and Frank Andrews, "Scientists in Organizations" (New York: John Wiley, 1966).

9. Charlan Jeanne Nemeth, "Managing Innovation: When Less Is More," *California Management Review* 40, 1 (Fall 1997).

10. Muzafer Sherif, et al., "Intergroup Conflict and Cooperation: The Robbers Cave Experiment" (Norman, Okla: University Book Exchange, 1961).

11. T. J. Watson, *A Business and Its Beliefs: The Ideas that Helped Build IBM* (New York: McGraw-Hill, 1963). Borrowing from the story by Danish philosopher Kierkegaard.

• **CHAPTER 5** •

1. As quoted by Teresa Amabile in the article "How to Kill Creativity," published in the *Harvard Business Review*, September-October 1998.

2. Albert Rothenberg. "Artistic Creation as Stimulated by Superimposed versus Combined Composite Visual Images," *Journal of Personality and Social Psychology* 50 (1986): 370-81.

3. S.H. Carson, J. B. Peterson, and D. M. Higgins, "Decreased Latent Inhibition Is Associated with Increased Creative Achieve-

ment in High-Functioning Individuals," *Journal of Personality and Social Psychology* 85, 3 (2003): 499-506.

4. Keith H. Hammonds, "How Google Grows . . . and Grows . . . and Grows," *Fast Company* 69 (April 2003). www.fastcompany .com/magazine/69/google.html

• CHAPTER 6 •

1. Jeff Mauzy and Richard Harriman, *Creativity, Inc.* (Boston: Harvard Business School Press, 2003).

2. Scott E. Page, "A Logic of Diversity," unpublished manuscript.

3. Ibid.

4. Mark Stefik and Barbara Stefik. *Stories and Strategies of Radical Innovation Breakthrough* (Cambridge, Mass.: MIT Press, 2004).

5. Ibid.

6. Ibid.

7. Reprinted with permission of Hasso Plattner. Originally from the article by Bruce Nussbaum, "The SAP School of Design." www .businessweek.com/innovate/content/oct2005/id20051003_610064 .htm

8. David A. Hounshell, *From the American System to Mass Production 1800-1932: The Development of Manufacturing Technology in the United States.* (Baltimore: The Johns Hopkins University Press, 1984).

9. *Source*: Jim Kardach. As published on the wireless networking magazine *Incisor* at www.click.co.uk/incisor.htm in online issues #34, 37, and 38 (2001).

10. Reprinted with permission of Paul MacCready.

11. Frans Johansson, *The Medicci Effect: Breakthrough Insights at the Intersection of Ideas, Concepts and Cultures"* (Boston: Harvard Business School Press, 2004).

12. Stefik and Stefik, *Stories and Strategies of Radical Innovation Breakthrough.*

13. National Institutes of Health website: www.grants.nih.gov/grants/guide/rfa-files/RFA-RM-04-008.html

14. Robert I. Sutton, *Weird Ideas That Work* (New York: The Free Press, 2002).

• CHAPTER 7 •

1. "Innovation: The New Reality for National Prosperity" (Draft Interim Report). Prepared for National Innovation Initiative by 21st Century Innovation Working Group, June 1, 2004.

2. I would like to acknowledge the contribution of Candis S. Cook of Synectics, Inc., in the categorization of the two types of roles outsiders can play: process and content.

3. Desiree de Myer, "Envision It: What's the Big Idea?" *Smart Business* Magazine, October 1, 2001, pp. 64-65.

4. Bruce Nussbaum, "The Power of Design," *BusinessWeek Online*, May 17, 2004.

5. Robert Cialdini, "The Perils of Being the Best and the Brightest," *Harvard Management Communication Newsletter*, May 1990.

6. Shelly Strom, "Designing an Experience." *Portland Business Journal*, April 29, 2005.

7. Some of the information for this story was found in the case study by Karen Freeze, "Umpqua Bank: Managing the Culture and Implementing the Brand," from the Case Study Research and Development Program at the Design Management Institute.

8. Tom Kelley. *The Ten Faces of Innovation: IDEO's Strategies for Beating the Devil's Advocate and Driving Creativity Throughout Your Organization* (New York: Currency/Doubleday, 2005).

9. Dean Takahashi, *Opening the X-Box: Inside Microsoft's Plan to Unleash an Entertainment Revolution* (Roseville, Calif.: Prima Publishing, 2002).

10. Joey Reiman, *Thinking for a Living: Creating Ideas That Revitalize Your Business, Career and Life.* (Atlanta, Ga.: Longstreet Press, 1998).

11. Dean 'Keith Simonton. *Origins of Genius: Darwinian Perspectives on Creativity* (Oxford: Oxford University Press, 1999).

12. D. Goleman and P. Kaufman, "The Art of Creativity," *Psychology Today.* www.cms.psychologytoday.com/articles/pto-1992 0301-000031.html

• CHAPTER 8 •

1. Santa Fe Institute website: www.santafe.edu/

2. *Science* 304, 5674 (May 21, 2004): 1117-1119.

3. Frans Johansson, *The Medicci Effect: Breakthrough Insights at the Intersection of Ideas, Concepts and Cultures* (Boston: Harvard Business School Press, 2004).

4. Committee on Facilitating Interdisciplinary Research Committee on Science, Engineering and Policy, "Facilitating Interdisciplinary Research" (The National Academies Press, 2005), p. 182. Corrected version of the quote by permission of Diane Rhoten.

5. Ibid.

6. John H. Lienhard, "Fessenden and Radio Sound" (from *Engines of Our Ingenuity* radio program, #1649). www.uh.edu/en gines/epi1649.htm.

• CHAPTER 9 •

1. Michael Michalko, *Cracking Creativity: The Secrets of Creative Genius.* (Berkeley, Calif.: Ten Speed Press, 1998).

2. Mark Stefik and Barbara Stefik, *Stories and Strategies of Radical Innovation Breakthrough* (Cambridge, Mass.: MIT Press, 2004).

3. Richard Watson, "Why You Can't Think Out of the Box When You're Sitting in One," FastCompany. www.fastcompany.com/ resources/innovation/watson/031405.html

4. Henri Poincaré, *The Foundations of Science—Science and*

Hypothesis: The Value of Science, Science and Method. Translated by G.B. Halstead (New York: Science Press, 1921).

5. Robert A. Guth, "Bill Gates Ponders High-Tech's Future at 'Think Weeks'; Seclusion in a Northwest Cabin Lets Microsoft's Boss Sort Promising Ideas," *Wall Street Journal,* as reprinted in the *Oregonian,* March 30, 2005, p. B3.

6. Committee on Facilitating Interdisciplinary Research Committee on Science, Engineering and Policy, "Facilitating Interdisciplinary Research" (The National Academies Press, 2005).

• CHAPTER 10 •

1. Barry Nalebuff and Ian Ayres, *Why Not? How to Use Everyday Ingenuity to Solve Problems Big and Small* (Boston: Harvard Business School Press, 2003).

2. Edward de Bono, *Six Thinking Hats* (New York: Little, Brown, 1985).

3. Ibid.

4. Michael Michalko, *Thinkertoys: A Handbook of Business Creativity* (Berkeley, Calif.: Ten Speed Press, 1991).

5. Steven Kotler, "7-Up Up and Away: Corporate Sponsorship, Civilian Astronauts and Inflatable Hotels Follow in X Prize's Jet Wash," *LA Weekly,* October 15-21, 2004.

6. From the transcript of the July 3, 2005 interview with Burt Rutan, broadcast on CBS Television's *60 Minutes.* www.cbsnews .com/stories/2005/06/30/60minutes/main705481.shtml

7. Based on e-mail correspondence with Burt Rutan. Published with permission of Burt Rutan.

8. From the website www.inventors.about.com/od/lstartinven tions/a/liquid_paper.htm

9. Innovation and Business Architectures, Inc., "The Innovation Imperative in Consumer Products." www.biz-architect.com/ innovation_imperative_consumer_products.htm

10. From the Australian Academy of Technological Sciences and Engineering Clunies Ross Foundation. www.storiesofinnovation.org/

11. *CMO* Magazine online resource: www.cmomagazine.com/read/090105/power-peril.html

12. *CIO* Magazine online resource: www.cio.com/research/surveyreport.cfm?id = 54

13. EBF Discussion Forum: www.ebfonline.com/debate/post.asp?id = 89

14. Richard Watson, "Why You Can't Think Out of the Box When You're Sitting in One," *FastCompany.* www.fastcompany.com/resources/innovation/watson/031405.html

15. Tom Field, "Unleash Innovation," *CIO* Magazine, August 15, 1999.

16. Michalko, *Thinkertoys.*

17. Morgan D. Jones, *The Thinker's Toolkit: 14 Powerful Techniques for Problem Solving* (New York: Random House, 1998).

18. Leigh Buchanan, "The Innovation Factor: A Field Guild to Innovation," *Inc.* Magazine, August 2002. www.inc.com/magazine/20020801/24451.html

19. *Deep Impact* (1998) was written by Bruce Joel Rubin and Michael Tolkin, and directed by Mimi Leder.

20. Teresa C. Brown, "Credit Union Honored for Babies at Work," *Pleasanton Weekly* online edition, December 5, 2003. www.pleasantonweekly.com/morgue/2003/2003_12_05.uncle05.shtml

• CHAPTER 11 •

1. Michael Lewis, *Moneyball: The Art of Winning an Unfair Game* (New York: W. W. Norton, 2004).

2. Ibid.

3. Mel Perel, "Corporate Courage: Breaking the Barrier to Innovation," Industrial Research Institute, May-June 2002.

4. *BusinessWeek,* "How to Learn Creativity and Innovation. www.businessweek.com/innovate/index.html

5. Clayton Christensen, *The Innovators Solution.* (Boston: Harvard Business School Press, 2003), p. 11.

6. Lou Lehr, dinner speech at the Wharton Entrepreneurial Center, University of Pennsylvania, 1979.

7. University of California at Berkeley, Haas School of Business Faculty Profiles, March 13, 2005. www.haas.berkeley.edu/news/faculty/Audia.html>

8. Charlan Jeanne Nemeth, "Managing Innovation: When Less Is More," *California Management Review* 40, 1 (Fall 1997).

9. Jeff Mauzy and Richard Harriman, *Creativity, Inc: Building an Inventive Organization* (Boston: Harvard Business School Press, 2003).

10. Pamela Tierney and Steven M. Farmer, "The Pygmalion Process and Employee Creativity," *Journal of Management* 30 (2004).

11. John Simons, "Therapy That Gets Inside Your Head—Literally," *Fortune* Magazine, June 13, 2005. www.fortune.com/fortune/subs/article/0,15114,1067053,00.html

NOTES

INDEX

· · · · · · · · · · ·